LEADING the
PROFESSIONALS

how to inspire & motivate professional service teams

Geoff Smith

**KOGAN
PAGE**

London and Sterling, VA

First published in Great Britain and the United States in 2004 by Kogan Page Limited.

120 Pentonville Road
London N1 9JN
UK
www.kogan-page.co.uk

22883 Quicksilver Drive
`Sterling VA 20166-2012
USA

© Geoff Smith, 2004

ISBN 0 7494 3996 3

British Library Cataloguing-in-Publication Data

A CIP record for this book is available from the British Library.

Library of Congress Cataloging-in-Publication Data

Smith, Geoff, 1938-
 Leading the professionals / Geoff Smith.
     p. cm.
Includes bibliographical references and index.
 ISBN 0-7494-3996-3
 1. Leadership. 2. Supervision of emplyees 3. Employee motivation.
4. Professional employees. 5. Personnel management. I. Title.
HD57. 7.S648 2003
658.4'092--dc22   2003021967

Typeset by Datamatics Technologies Ltd., Mumbai, INDIA
Printed and bound in Great Britain by Cambrian Printers Ltd,
Aberystwyth,Wales

Contents

About the author

After working at the Ford Motor Company, Geoff Smith spent a large part of his career at the Ashridge Business School. In addition to his teaching he was a member of the management committee for much of his time, first with responsibility for the client relations activity and subsequently as Director of Studies. In his early days at Ashridge he was responsible for developing the tailor-made course business. In the late 1980s he was seconded to The Thomson Corporation for two years. He worked for professional publishing companies and contributed to policy making and planning at director level as well as managing a number of marketing projects.

He is co-author of *Personnel Administration and Industrial Relations*. He has a degree in economics and is a Fellow of the Chartered Institute of Personnel and Development.

Most of his current work is with professional service firms where he helps to improve performance by facilitating strategy discussions, coaching individuals and running learning sets and leadership workshops.

If you have any comments or questions he can be contacted at: geoffsmith@mtd.uk.com or by telephone at +44 (0)1296 747041.

Acknowledgements

Many thanks to the following who have helped me to write the book:

My wife, Andrea, for her unstinting support and encouragement, for lots of help with preparing the manuscript and for making me express myself more clearly.

Bill Braddick, Ann-Frances Kinsler, Aimee Luther, Peter McArthur, Derek Saunders, Guy Smith, Helen Smith and Tom Welch, who all generously gave their time to read the draft manuscript. They each gave me invaluable feedback.

The many friends, colleagues, clients and participants at workshops and seminars who have helped to shape my thoughts about leadership over the years.

Those individuals mentioned in the text who offered valuable insights and permission to quote them: Tim Aspinall, Alison Chadwick, Richard Collier-Keywood, John Cridland, Cheryl Giovannoni, Robert Halton, Jonathan Hood, Denzil Jones, Digby Jones, Nigel Knowles, David Law, Chris Lucas, John Martin, Ian Pearman, Richard Sexton, Paul Sharp, Ed Smith, Tim Solomon and John Stapleton.

The Confederation of British Industry, DLA, DMH and PricewaterhouseCoopers for permission to reproduce extracts from documentation.

Louise Cameron and Pauline Goodwin of Kogan Page for their helpful advice and guidance.

Yvonne Booth for designing the book cover.

Angela Briscoe for patiently preparing an early draft of the typescript.

Introduction

The golden rule is there are no golden rules.
— (George Bernard Shaw)

The ways in which people go about their business in, say, law and accountancy firms, advertising agencies, design businesses, architectural practices and television production units are clearly very different. It requires no more than a cursory glance to detect significant cultural differences. The team leaders in these organizations, although having distinct professional mindsets and perceptions, nevertheless face similar challenges. Owing to the nature of their work and training, many professionals prefer to do things in their own way. They are knowledge workers or conceptualists who rely heavily on their own expertise. Wherever they work they seek both to use and to expand the existing knowledge base. Although they usually have to work in teams they are often unenthusiastic about it. They certainly resist being over-managed. The challenge for their leaders is to foster and maintain well-coordinated, high-performing teams capable of achieving clear business objectives, but with a light touch. It is about encouraging and supporting rather than directing and controlling. The

French verb *animer* (to run, spur on, stage, host, present, liven up, put a sparkle into and lead), for which there is no precise English equivalent, sums up the task neatly.

Digby Jones, Director-General of the Confederation of British Industry (CBI) and formerly senior partner at one of Britain's largest law firms, explains the dilemma:

> I believe that leadership of professional teams is much the same as team leading in other walks of life. It brings similar responsibilities and requires similar skills. However, from my experience as a lawyer and senior partner and latterly here at the CBI where we have a number of professional teams working on business critical policy issues, leading professionals can be much tougher than many people realise.
>
> Professional people generally have had a rigorous training before they start working and they tend to have a sceptical turn of mind. They enjoy challenging received wisdom and trying to reach a consensus is often quite difficult. Many of them prefer to work alone so getting teams to work together can be a tough proposition. The bottom line is that professionals value their independence and judgement so their team leaders usually have to work doubly hard, often in quite subtle ways to achieve accountability.
>
> Perhaps the best leaders of professional teams lead gently with no sign of a heavy hand. They are good at helping their people to think through problems and are always available. Although they are good at stimulating enthusiasm it is done in a rather understated, low-key way. They also do all the usual things like promoting teamwork, morale boosting, maintaining standards and encouraging everyone to pull together for a common purpose but they do them almost without being noticed. It is not easy. Clearly, very good inter-personal skills are necessary but that is not enough. It also requires a very positive and determined state of mind to enjoy getting the best out of other people and self-discipline is a must.

If you are, or are about to become, a team leader of professionals then this book is for you. It is a practical guide to the basics of leading in a professional setting. It is not about theory. Most of the thoughts and suggestions derive from observations of how the best leaders of professionals behave in practice. Consequently the tone of the chapter and section headings, and much of the content, sounds prescriptive. However, I suggest that you treat the recommendations as possibilities that may be worth trying out. Why not keep George Bernard Shaw's maxim in mind? Why not experiment with those leadership ideas that appeal? If they work for you then that is well and good. If not, abandon them and try something else.

Teams may be located in partnerships providing professional services on a commercial basis. They may be within large corporations or in public sector bodies, providing services internally to colleagues. They may be in trade or employers' associations. They may be contributing to voluntary organizations. Most of the illustrations, examples and quotations in the book relate to partnerships in Britain. For convenience, therefore, the word 'firm' is used throughout to represent organizations within which professionals work. I believe, though, that many of the issues discussed are just as relevant to professional service team leaders elsewhere. I hope, also, that professionals working outside Britain may find something of value.

I recommend that you read the book straight through since the concepts in the later chapters are built on ideas explored earlier. Part One is concerned with the basics. It covers the links between leadership and management; the importance of self-awareness for effective leadership; the roles and responsibilities of team leaders; and how to find sufficient time to do the leadership work.

Part Two deals with the major tasks involved in being a high-performing professional service team leader. These are providing direction and leading change; communicating well; creating the conditions for people to be well motivated; coaching colleagues so that they can improve their performance and adapt to new demands; fostering teamwork; coping with difficulties and crises; and assessing results.

Part Three explores the particular responsibilities that team leaders have for bringing new people on board. The tasks involved in selecting, inducting and nurturing newcomers are explored.

Part Four is for those leaders who, from time to time, may find themselves running temporary project teams, in addition to leading their regular groups of colleagues.

Part Five covers influencing skills, which are important not only for leading team members but also for dealing with clients and representing the interests of the team in the firm.

Finally in Part Six a number of familiar leadership problems are posed. The opportunity is given for you to compare your own solutions with my suggestions. It is by way of being a summary of the main points.

Part One

Basics

1

Leadership, management and self-awareness

We are what we repeatedly do.
Excellence then, is not an act, but a habit.

— (Aristotle)

When professionals such as lawyers, architects, engineers, accountants, advertising specialists, designers, teachers and research scientists become team leaders they invariably have to continue with their technical work. They have to combine the roles of team leader and team player. They also have to manage individuals who expect and enjoy considerable autonomy and who often prefer to work alone rather than with colleagues. Professionals, whether they work for professional service firms or within other private or public sector organizations, tend to be unenthusiastic about being managed. They prefer to do things in their own way without reference to the ideas and views of colleagues. Inspiring, motivating, coaching and managing bright knowledge workers, in such circumstances, is difficult and rather different from the leadership challenges that people face in other walks of life.

Ed Smith, UK Board Member at the international business advisory services firm PricewaterhouseCoopers, sums up the difficulties:

> A professional partnership brings together people with strong personalities who usually want to shape their worlds and, in many ways, have a deep-down preference for being sole traders. We are experts in our fields, spending much of our time advising our clients, and many of us don't particularly recognize the connectivity which leadership tries to bring to our specialist skills.

There are two common problems. First, the belief that professionals cannot be led and managed takes root. A mythology that professionals do not like working in teams, resist accountability, always know best, are uninterested in broader business issues outside their own speciality and are reluctant to be helped becomes entrenched. As a result, team leaders are often no more than nominal heads of groups who undertake a number of additional administrative and clerical tasks.

The second problem arises partly from the first. Professionals are frequently reluctant to take on a leadership role. Some of them believe that they cannot make a difference. For others it is because they enjoy being designers, lawyers, teachers, accountants and scientists. That was the career, after all, that they were trained for, and they see a leadership role as a distraction. Yet others worry that if they were to become a team leader they would begin to lose touch with their professional work, become out of date and ultimately risk career damage or even job loss.

I will try to show that, far from giving in to these difficulties, considerable benefits can accrue from having well-led, highly competent and motivated teams of professionals working together towards common objectives. This in principle is no different from what is required in successful organizations generally. However, because of the nature of professional work and of professional people, the task requires considerable sensitivity. Leaders of professionals have little power or authority by virtue of their positions alone. They are largely, but not entirely, leading and managing peers and colleagues rather than subordinates, staff or employees.

Ed Smith at PricewaterhouseCoopers puts this into context:

> Our team leaders only succeed by being excellent facilitators and enablers. They do a lot of leading by listening and providing help to their people so that they can live up to their capabilities. We put coaching at the centre of the team leadership role. There is a continuing need to help people to hone their

relationship skills so that they can operate with ease at board level with their clients. Coaching also involves knowledge transfer and helping people to cope with changing circumstances. Sometimes it is demonstrating best practice. It is also about helping team members to develop their careers and to continue to learn.

Good leadership in our firm is not particularly a matter of drama and charisma. There is a lot of one-to-one work. An immense amount of consultation and dialogue with team members and support for them is involved. In a way we have a reverse pyramid. The unit leaders and their teams throughout the firm hold up the partnership from below.

The CBI employs highly qualified young policy analysts and advisers who prepare papers on political, economic, social and technological issues that are important to member firms. They also lobby ministers, politicians and civil servants on such matters. Some of the analysts and advisers are generalists and others are specialists such as economists, lawyers and environmental experts. They work both in dedicated specialist teams and in multidisciplinary project teams.

John Cridland, Deputy Director-General at the CBI, has this to say about the challenges involved in leading these teams of professionals:

We select our young policy advisers primarily for their intellect, creativity and ability to make individual contributions. We don't want identikit people. We want them to be different and original. In many ways, in organizational terms, they resemble old-fashioned craftsmen rather than modern team players. They demand and expect independence and in many ways that is a good thing. The downside is that sometimes a touch of intellectual arrogance creeps in. Our leaders have the difficult task of fostering individual intellectual excellence whilst at the same time ensuring that team members meet the CBI's service standards such as prompt, polite and comprehensive replies to questions from members. The team leaders are first among equals. They need to encourage, support, cajole and occasionally confront but not to direct or instruct. Our culture is mixed. It is partly collegiate but we have to put some iron into the staffroom atmosphere because we are interested in objectives, performance standards, customer care and so on.

All of our team leaders play a significant role in scoping assignments and setting objectives along with each of their team members. The problem is that sometimes it ends there in that the person doing the job is left to get on with it. Some of our leaders feel that they cannot intervene, even if things are going wrong. They feel that to get further involved would smack of supervising and that would be considered unprofessional. Our best leaders, on the other hand, do not let go completely. They gently help the person doing the job to steer the assignment around to get it back on track. Although I have stressed the encouragement of individual excellence we also want our people to share their thinking, provide each other with ideas, give each other support and so on. These are conventional teamworking attributes. Our teams now work in open-plan offices to help that along. Our opposite numbers in the German employers' associations are astonished. They all have individual cell offices and would deeply resist any attempt to change. Although the open-plan office helps, it remains, in my view, very much the task of our team leaders to foster good teamwork and to balance that with nudging people along to become outstanding individual contributors. It is both/and rather than either/or.

There is a tricky issue involved here. As well as having the necessary skills, those chosen to be leaders of professional service teams need to be genuinely enthusiastic about the task of helping others to perform effectively. Creating the conditions for people to be highly motivated to achieve first-class results and have the competence to do so is a key requirement of the job. It is therefore crucial for firms to signal the importance of leadership by communicating the fact that it is a highly valued activity and by rewarding those who do it well. This may seem a trite point. However, I have come across too many professional service environments where the leadership function is poorly regarded. It is viewed disparagingly when compared with the professional work itself. Consequently individuals with no enthusiasm for the job are pushed into team leadership positions with deplorable results. They often have excellent qualities such as being outstanding at their technical work and very good with clients. But they do not lead well because they are reluctant to do the job. Either they do not see it as being sufficiently important or they would rather be doing something else.

LEAD AND MANAGE – TEAM LEADERS NEED TO DO BOTH

Table 1.1 illustrates the more common management and leadership activities that leaders of professional teams undertake. It will be evident

Table 1.1 Management and leadership activities

Typical Management Activities	Typical Leadership Activities
Making short-term plans.	Getting team members to provide their ideas on direction, objectives and strategies.
Acquiring and allocating resources.	Leading by example.
Getting the right people into the right jobs.	Communicating and enthusing people about the agreed direction, objectives and strategies.
Seeing that policies, procedures and systems are observed.	Inspiring people to overcome obstacles and to try new ways of working.
Providing authority and encouraging responsibility.	Creating the conditions where people will be motivated to achieve outstanding results.
Monitoring performance.	Coaching people to help them to change and to perform more effectively.
Coping with disciplinary issues. Resolving conflicts.	Fostering teamwork.

that both leading and managing are important for continuing success. Good leaders cope effectively with the management basics. They also have the skills to enthuse others to change, get a team to work together, secure agreement on key issues and inspire by example. It is useful, however, to make a distinction between management and leadership for two reasons. The first is that management is a crucial function in ensuring that short-term high-quality results are delivered. Good leadership is essential for achieving change and for keeping up the momentum of first-class performance over the long run. The second reason arises from answers that I get from professionals when I ask whether leadership and management are seen as strengths or weaknesses in their firms. Usually I learn that management skills appear to be stronger, in general, than leadership attributes. The reason given is that, for many professionals, the combination of temperament and training seems to equip them to cope more easily and successfully with their technical work and management responsibilities than with their leadership challenges. Many professionals have to work quite hard, therefore, to cultivate the leadership skills that are needed if they are going to be successful team leaders.

One firm that bears out the belief that there is a high correlation between being a good employer and outstanding performance, which implies having good leadership and management at all levels, is DLA. It is a highly successful law firm. It has enjoyed exceptional fee income and profit growth during the last few years. It has won a string of awards including Law Firm of the Year and European Firm of the Year in 2002. There have been awards also for its human resources strategy. It was rated highly in the *Sunday Times* 100 Best Companies to Work For in 2001, 2002 and 2003. Over the last six years, DLA's image in the legal marketplace has changed from being an organization with a 'rottweiler culture' and a 'revolving door' to that of 'a good place to work'.

This is what DLA's Nigel Knowles, Managing Partner of the Year in 2002, has to say about leadership and management:

> An aligned and successful business which gets big and old can suffer from inertia, which does not matter too much when markets are stable but can be disastrous when markets shift. We can all think of companies that have suffered this fate. In my view it is because, although they may have been well managed, there was a failure of leadership.
>
> Managing is all about planning, budgeting, organizing, staffing and controlling. People who just manage are not agents of change. Leadership is about having a clear direction, aligning, communicating, motivating and inspiring. Leaders are agents of change. Because the world is changing fast we need leaders at all levels to maintain a competitive advantage.
>
> A firm's ultimate success will be based on its capability to innovate. In a professional service firm this can happen at three levels. At the grass roots you must have a large number of incremental improvements in service and working prac- tices. At the next level you must have a number of new initia- tives and new products. At the top of the firm you must have one or two big bets, for example going international or making a major acquisition.
>
> This clearly scotches the rumour that it is only the people at the top, whoever they are, who can make things happen. Leaders at all levels must take responsibility for innovation and change.
>
> In our business we encourage team leaders to be good at both leading and managing. Both are important. However, we probably have to work a bit harder to get them to be really good at the leadership stuff. Leaders need to have passion. They can't think their way into change but rather they have to see and feel the need for change. It is seeing and feeling that stirs the emotions and makes people passionate about whatever it is they want to do.

Team leaders in all firms need to be good at leading and managing. Tim Solomon, Managing Partner at the London office of advertising agency Ogilvy & Mather, explains its importance in his business:

The starting point is our need to have people throughout the firm who have a well-developed entrepreneurial spirit. Our clients appreciate us much more if we are on the front foot, always looking for new opportunities and coming up with possible solutions. For this to happen we need team leaders who are really good with words, who can articulate a clear sense of direction and who can inspire their team colleagues to stretch themselves to support the brands that they are working for. The ability to provide a clear vocal message, which is in tune with people's thinking but also enthuses them to take the extra step, is paramount. The best of our team leaders encourage inventive mavericks but discourage prima donnas and office politicians. They foster curiosity, candour, originality, perseverance, vigour and civility. They require commitment to the highest possible professional standards but they also expect people to deal with each other with kindness. There need be no conflict between these aims. Lastly, our team leaders would not be up to the job if they were not administratively competent. Strong capability in resource and capacity planning and cost control, for example, is essential.

So, in my opinion, our leaders need to have an interesting mixture of skills. They have to be able to encourage enterprising individualism whilst at the same time getting people to work well together. They also need to be able to surround these leadership attributes with skilful administrative management. We are generally able to identify people with the potentiality to become team leaders through the ways in which they work with clients and colleagues. If they are good at relationships and are able, positively, to influence others then they will probably make good team leaders. If they manage their time and assignments well then these are indicators of a broader management capability. We then develop these skills through a mixture of in-house coaching and the use of training programmes.

For those readers who wish to develop their leadership attributes, a good starting point is to undertake some basic self-analysis. One way to do that is to use the concept of emotional intelligence popularized by Daniel Goleman in his book of that name published in 1995. The term 'emotional intelligence' is used to describe the degree to which we are able to empathize with others and be skilful socially, be resilient in the face of obstacles, be persistent, be well motivated and control our impulses. It also, crucially, includes the extent of our self-awareness. Our emotional intelligence can be strengthened and nourished. Why not have a go at judging yourself against the qualities listed in the boxes

INTRAPERSONAL QUALITIES ASSOCIATED WITH EMOTIONAL INTELLIGENCE

Self-awareness

▌ Am I aware of the effects of my behaviour on others?

▌ Am I realistic in my assessment of my abilities?

▌ Am I realistic in my assessment of my moods and emotions?

▌ Do I recognize feelings as being valuable?

▌ Is my self-confidence well judged?

Emotional self-control

▌ Am I able to control my emotions?

▌ Am I able to avoid suppressing my feelings when it is more appropriate for them to be expressed?

Self-regulation

▌ Am I conscientious about such matters as fulfilling obligations, helping others, collaborating and realizing objectives?

▌ Am I able to control or redirect impulses?

▌ Am I able to organize my work and time effectively?

Flexibility

▌ Am I adaptable when necessary?

▌ Do I enjoy new experiences and variety?

▮ Am I open to new ideas?

▮ Do I enjoy being with individuals who are very different from me?

Motivation

▮ Am I able to pursue objectives with energy and enthusiasm?

▮ Do I have a strong drive to achieve good results?

▮ Am I generally optimistic about achieving success?

Resilience

▮ Am I persistent in pursuit of my objectives?

▮ Am I self-sufficient?

▮ Am I persistent when faced by obstacles?

▮ Am I resourceful when faced by challenges?

Well-being

▮ Am I optimistic generally about the future?

▮ Do I use coping mechanisms for dealing with tension, eg physical exercise, talking to others or taking time out to relax?

▮ Do I keep myself physically and mentally in reasonably good shape?

INTERPERSONAL QUALITIES ASSOCIATED WITH EMOTIONAL INTELLIGENCE

Social skill

■ Am I proficient in building relationships?

■ Am I at ease socially?

■ Am I self-assured?

■ Do I respond with warmth to others?

■ Am I able to build trust?

■ Do I communicate orally with ease?

Empathy

■ Am I able to see, and demonstrate that I see, the world from the perspective of others?

■ Am I aware of social nuances?

■ Am I sensitive towards the feelings of others?

Energy

■ Do I display commitment to others by getting on with the job, helping, joining in, offering ideas and being enthusiastic?

■ Do I seek feedback from others about my performance?

■ Can I make things happen in a forceful but sensitive way?

■ Am I lively and responsive in my relationships with others?

■ Am I energized by new challenges?

■ Can I maintain the impetus with others on relatively routine activities?

Persuasiveness

■ Am I able generally to make a good impression with others?

■ Am I good at seeking other people's points of view?

■ Am I able to offer ideas in a non-defensive fashion?

■ Am I good at problem solving in collaboration with colleagues?

■ Am I able to influence others by doing?

Tolerance

■ Am I visibly patient with the beliefs and values of others?

■ Am I fair-minded about ideas and possibilities?

■ Do I communicate respect and regard for others during conflicts?

'Intrapersonal qualities associated with emotional intelligence' and 'Interpersonal qualities associated with emotional intelligence'?

It is likely that you will score well in some of them and for others there will be room for improvement. Capitalizing on your strengths and consciously seeking to do better on the others is a good starting point for enhancing your leadership abilities.

You might like to ask your team members or colleagues to give their views as to how well you measure up to the qualities listed. Getting feedback from others is a very good way for us to learn about ourselves. However, it is a good idea to prepare the ground carefully before engaging in an exercise of this sort.

In some organizations the process of providing feedback to team leaders is formalized as part of what is known as 360-degree feedback (individuals receive assessments of their behaviour from their team members, their peers and their seniors). Usually forms are completed anonymously, the results are averaged by an independent agency, for example the human resource people or outside consultants, and the results are subsequently fed back to the individuals concerned.

My preference is for team leaders to seek feedback from their colleagues informally through conversation. Indeed for leaders to behave in this way is evidence in itself of emotional intelligence. It is likely to lead to greater self-awareness and it will help to build trust. It is, of course, difficult and unwise for someone who has never sought feedback from others suddenly to request detailed assessments of behaviour in relation to the qualities listed in the boxes. Colleagues, and especially team members, are unlikely to be very revealing until a high level of trust has been established. It is probably better to start by asking some low-risk questions that are less likely to cause discomfort or resistance. You could for example begin by enquiring whether your colleagues feel that you are available when needed or whether you provide help sufficiently when it is required. As confidence and trust increase it then becomes possible to seek more detailed assessments of behaviour with a reasonable likelihood of receiving some useful feedback. The process of giving and receiving feedback is explored in more detail in Chapters 6 and 7.

DEVELOP YOUR INTERPERSONAL AND INTRAPERSONAL SKILLS

For many people a lot of the interpersonal and intrapersonal skills come naturally. Good leaders build on their strengths. However, there are usually some forms of behaviour that need to be changed and others that may need to be engaged in more often. Table 1.2 provides a simple checklist of action points that might be helpful to those wishing to enhance particular qualities associated with emotional intelligence.

It is perhaps helpful at this stage to be clear that behaviour is not the same thing as personality. People often make the erroneous assumption that they are the same. Behaviour is what we do, for example laughing, talking, listening, driving, playing sport, drafting documents, running meetings, conducting negotiations or watching television. Behaviour is action and is directly observable and it can be changed. Personality traits are deep-seated preferences for the ways in which we use our minds, focus our attention and draw energy. Extraverts, for example, prefer to focus on the outer world of people and activity. They draw their energy from interacting with people and from taking action. Introverts, on the other hand, prefer to direct their attention to the inner world of ideas and experiences. They draw their energy from reflecting on thoughts, memories and feelings. Whilst personality preferences clearly predispose people to behave in particular ways and set very broad limits, they leave us with plenty of scope when it comes to ways of behaving. For instance, we all know introverts who are capable of making entertaining after-dinner speeches and extraverts who are outstanding listeners.

Some people use their personalities as an excuse for being unwilling to change behaviour. We are all familiar with the saying, 'A leopard can't change its spots'. In fact, whilst it is true that our basic personalities are relatively fixed (except in response to brain damage, brainwashing or the use of drugs), it is possible for us to make significant changes to our behaviour if we so wish.

Table 1.2 Changing behaviour

Qualities	Some Action to Take to Become More Competent if Necessary
Self-awareness	Seek feedback from colleagues and team members. Share thinking about personal strengths and weaknesses with one or two respected colleagues.
Emotional self-control	Analyse causes of loss of control and explore possible coping tactics with a close friend. Express disappointment or annoyance rather than anger. When hindered by an unwanted feeling, ask yourself 'How can I use the present time more effectively?' Try to develop the belief that nothing is important enough to justify losing control. Acknowledge that people are fallible. Count to 10 before responding.
Self-regulation	Set aside time routinely for setting clear goals, prioritizing and planning work before taking action. Review tasks undertaken to learn and modify if necessary when engaged in similar activities subsequently.
Flexibility	Make a point of getting involved in brainstorming sessions with colleagues and team members. Encourage team members to offer ideas. Make the effort to meet and talk to people from different walks of life.

(*continued*)

Table 1.2 (*continued*)

Qualities	Some Action to Take to Become More Competent if Necessary
Motivation	Ensure that your goals are challenging but also attainable. Try to ensure that at least 75 per cent of your work is interesting, enjoyable, fun or intrinsically satisfying.
Resilience	Ensure that you are mentally and physically in good shape by making time for regular physical exercise, relaxation and mental stimulation.
Well-being	The same action points as for resilience.
Social skill	Seek out situations where you have to interact with others. Devote more time to small talk. Learn how to make good presentations, practise with video recordings and obtain feedback from others. Provide time for conversations with colleagues and team members. Build trust by keeping people fully informed. Give full attention when listening. Listen as much as talk in social encounters. Use people's names more frequently (but avoid it being mechanical or inappropriately familiar). Make occasional amusing remarks against yourself. Don't interrupt. Ask more questions (but in a warm and friendly way). Smile.
Empathy	In conversations make a point of demonstrating that you can see situations from the other person's point of view. Read a book on personality differences to provide a framework for understanding the different ways that people feel and see the world around them. Never assume that other people automatically see situations in the same way that you do. Be prepared to explore feelings that underpin behaviour. Show personal interest. Express support for the efforts that others make. Show that you are listening attentively by reflecting back, asking questions sensitively and summarizing.
Energy	Seek feedback regularly from others about performance. Tackle collaborative exercises, for example in meetings, with enthusiasm. Show keen interest in others. Respond with vigour. Behave with enthusiasm even when you don't feel like it – eventually it becomes second nature. Be lively and enthusiastic in encounters with others.
Persuasiveness	Learn how to make good presentations, practise with video

	recordings and obtain feedback from others.

recordings and obtain feedback from others.

Listen attentively by reflecting back, asking questions sensitively and summarizing.

Take part in idea generation and problem solving in meetings with colleagues and team members.

Lead by example.

Tolerance   Listen attentively to different opinions and don't rush to disagree.

Don't interrupt.

Acknowledge that you understand the different values and beliefs that others may have.

In conflict situations show respect and regard for others by avoiding personal attacks and emotive language.

Stick to the issues and express your understanding of other people's positions.

Try to solve conflicts by cooperation rather than competition.

Give a fair hearing to other people's ideas and proposals.

A PEN PORTRAIT OF A TEAM LEADER WITH STRONG EMOTIONAL INTELLIGENCE

Everybody who works in Gillian Beresford's team agrees that she is a fine leader. 'She is not perfect but then nobody is,' says one colleague, 'but she is always willing to learn.' Her team members talk in glowing terms about her enthusiasm for the job and for her colleagues. Whether she is greeting somebody for the first time in the morning, having a discussion about a work-related topic or running a meeting, there is a visible display of energy, good humour and full attention to others. Her colleagues have many very positive things to say about her. Here are some examples:

■ 'She takes a genuine interest in our lives. It is definitely not mechanical and routine as it is with some people. She comes back with questions and comments when something important is going on.'

■ 'She is always straight with us. If things are going well she always thanks us for our particular contributions. It is really meant because she rarely resorts to vague comments. If there are problems with our work she is always upfront and explains what is wrong. However, the great thing is that she then gives us some help. She has a marvellous ability to help us to think things through by asking questions and giving support.'

▌ 'I would describe her as a person with real integrity. She doesn't take credit for other people's good ideas. She doesn't blame others when things go wrong.'

▌ 'Gillian doesn't lose her cool when we have a crisis. We are all encouraged to work things through systematically. She seems to believe that her most important job, as team leader, is to help us overcome difficulties and sort out problems.'

▌ 'She has time for us: time for us personally and time for our work. She is a fantastic listener. You don't feel that her mind is somewhere else. You just know that she is paying full attention.'

▌ 'When I am running up against big problems she seems to understand what they are and more importantly how I am feeling. She is not a softy, she doesn't let anybody off the hook but she does go out of her way to help with putting things right. I usually feel a lot better after a conversation with her. I have never had a boss before that I can say that about.'

▌ 'I think that one of the more remarkable things about her is that she asks us for our views about her work as team leader. She likes to know how she is doing. At first I was a bit reticent about speaking up but I feel that I can be honest with her because I trust her and I trust her because she is always honest with me. It is easier for all of us to own up to shortcomings and seek help because she is very willing, herself, to admit that she has lots to learn.'

▌ 'You have the impression that Gillian really likes her colleagues. It can't be possible for her to like everything about everybody but she definitely has the knack of finding something good in all of us. You feel that there is a genuine warmth.'

▌ 'I admire her most of all because she invariably meets her obligations to clients and to us. It is tremendous leadership by example. She is well organized and almost always on time.'

▌ 'She encourages our opinions and ideas not only on the technical details of our work but also on our relationships with clients, on how we work together, how to improve systems and on how to get more business. She does this with everybody including the secretaries in the team.'

■ 'She is very tolerant of other people's views and listens well to differences of opinion. Even with those that she disagrees with there is no personal animosity. In disagreements she sticks to the issues and avoids personality bashing.'

■ 'She expects high standards. I appreciate that but even more I appreciate the encouragement and support that she gives us all in living up to those high standards.'

■ 'She seems to lead steadily. There is a very positive mood in our team for most of the time. We know what is expected of us. Indeed we contribute our thoughts to those expectations. We get on with things with the right amount of encouragement and the right amount of prodding. If we don't meet target dates, however, there is some explaining to do.'

■ 'I think that we are a well-motivated bunch because we all enjoy our work and we are successful on the whole. However, we have our down moments. Gillian is able to transmit her own get-up-and-go and dedication to us on those occasions. I suppose it is because when things are not going as well as they should we do a bit of problem solving together, and help each other; then the motivation returns.'

■ 'The thing that I like about her is that she is optimistic about things. Even in difficult times she seems to be able to take a positive view and to find opportunities to explore with us. That's quite uplifting.'

■ 'Gillian doesn't let things fester. If there are problems between people in the team she seems to learn about them very quickly. She talks to the people concerned and helps them to come to some sort of agreement to put things right. Usually everybody comes away feeling that some useful progress has been made.'

∎ 'Although she is a hard worker and expects us to be the same there is an easy atmosphere in the team. There is plenty of humour and good fun as part of the day's work.'

∎ 'The thing that I like about Gillian is that she is very responsive to our ideas. She listens and is willing for us to try something new if it appeals. If for some reason we can't follow through then she gives good explanations. She also provides time in meetings for a bit of brainstorming and encourages everybody to voice their ideas.'

∎ 'Gillian is very sensitive to feelings and is not afraid to explore them with us if she thinks that will help us to do a better job together.'

∎ 'She is almost too good to be true. Having thought about it I have come to the conclusion that whilst some of it comes naturally I feel quite sure that she has also schooled herself to be a good team leader. She takes her leadership responsibilities as seriously as she takes her personal professional work. You have to make a real effort to be a good leader, in my view, and that is what she has done.'

∎ 'We all play a part in setting the team's objectives and developing the business plan which follows. We have a lot of good-natured battles during our discussions. Once everything is decided Gillian keeps us on track for what we have agreed to do.'

Do you know a team leader with similar characteristics to Gillian? If so, you have an excellent role model.

2

What leaders of professionals do: An overview

Although Henry Miller's words are an oversimplification, there is more than a grain of truth in what he says, particularly as far as leaders of professionals are concerned. Leadership is an enabling and facilitating rather than a directing and controlling role. A gentle blend of nudging people in the right direction, ideally agreed beforehand with those involved, and the provision of help and support when needed generally works well. Peter Drucker, the eminent thinker on business, leadership and management, notes that 'knowledge-based organisations' are 'composed largely of specialists who direct and discipline their own performance through organised feedback from colleagues and customers' (1989). The watchwords, therefore, are leading with a light touch.

Leaders of professional service teams have sometimes been likened to conductors of orchestras whose job is both to coach musicians and to inspire them to excel. But there are weaknesses in this analogy because many conductors, it seems, over-manage. Conductors often directly supervise the activities of a large number of musicians, right down to small details. Power and authority are considerable and are frequently displayed. Benjamin Zander, conductor of the Boston Philharmonic Orchestra, who sees himself as much more a coach than a maestro, was once asked if the conductor of the orchestra is a good model for leadership in the business world. His response was damning: 'It's the worst! The conductor is the last bastion of totalitarianism in the world – the person whose authority never gets questioned. There's a saying: every dictator aspires to be a conductor.' Benjamin Zander tells a story about the maestro Toscanini (Zander and Zander, 2000):

> It is said that once in the middle of a rehearsal, in a fit of anger, he fired a longstanding member of the double bass section, who now had to return home to tell his wife that he was out of a job. As the bass player packed up his instrument, he mentioned a few things that he had hitherto kept to himself and, as he left the hall for the final time, shouted at Toscanini 'You are a no-good son of a bitch'. So oblivious was Toscanini to the notion that a player would dare to challenge his authority that he waved back 'It is too late to apologise!'

Benjamin Zander has reinterpreted the conductor's role. He sees his job primarily as one of enabling the musicians to bring the best out of themselves. He believes one of his main functions is to coach musicians to be expressive performers of great music. He says (Zander and Zander, 2000):

> One way I know if I am performing well is to look into my musicians' eyes. The eyes never lie. If the eyes are shining, then I know that my leadership is working. Human beings in the presence of possibility react physically as well as emotionally. If the eyes aren't shining, I ask myself, 'What am I doing that's keeping my musicians' eyes from shining?'

It looks as though Benjamin Zander's style is a rather better model for leading professional teams than the example of the more conventional conductor of the orchestra.

BE SPECIFIC ABOUT ENDS
AND ALLOW DISCRETION ABOUT MEANS

THE WHAT AND THE HOW OF LEADERSHIP

Be clear about the ends – the what

The leader's task is to provide clear, persistent statements of the direction, goals and values of the firm and the team.

Allow discretion about the means – the how

The leader's task is to empower professionals and support people in the team on implementation and action. This involves:

- developing more and better skills so that they can handle more responsibility;
- getting everyone to contribute their ideas;
- giving people more discretion rather than less;
- fostering a climate of trust that is built on openness and honesty.

Studies of effective leaders are remarkably consistent. Good leaders are specific about 'ends' and allow discretion about 'means'; this notion is illustrated in the box 'The what and the how of leadership'.

At international business advisory services firm Pricewaterhouse-Coopers, team leaders are clear about the ends and allow discretion about the means. Partners Richard Collier-Keywood, David Law, Chris Lucas and Richard Sexton describe their approaches to this aspect of leadership.

Richard Collier-Keywood says:

> I get ideas from my colleagues and then paint the vision of where we need to get to. It is my job then to sell the vision to the team. I really have to believe in it otherwise I can't sell it. Team members have plenty of freedom then to work out how to achieve the goals. My job at this stage is to support implementation and check performance at intervals – milestones – to ensure that we are on track.

In a similar vein David Law observes:

> My colleagues contribute their thinking to the business plan. I coordinate the ideas and publish a short document on our

vision and values, aspirations and performance targets. I talk to everybody about this. People are then free to get on with the job as they wish as long as they follow some basic disciplines like completing the time sheets and so long as they don't betray trust. It's my job to create the right environment. If I do that well then, with professional people, everything else should follow.

Chris Lucas describes the approach in this way:

It's my job to paint a picture of the direction for the business including collective and individual actions and projects. I need to draft or colour our team's vision having listened to what my colleagues have to say and having taken account of the over-all objectives of PricewaterhouseCoopers UK. I then sell the vision back to the team. There is regular reinforcement. I keep plugging away at the message at meetings, one to one and in performance appraisals. People then get on with the job. There is no micromanagement but I do monitor to make sure that the projects are coming in on time, that the billing is timely and that the cash is collected.

Richard Sexton says:

I mustn't try to do people's jobs. Our people are highly talented professionals. I see it as my task to set the tone, get the environment right and point the business in the right direction. I have to give leadership on what needs to be done and on the way we should behave towards clients and colleagues. I have to interpret the PricewaterhouseCoopers corporate vision for the local level, take account of the thinking of my team colleagues and then create our own vision and goals. I then bang the drum about these things in meetings and with individuals. Accountants are very analytical and critical. They are good at telling people what won't work. I see my job as mainly getting our team members into a 'can do' mood. So I talk about our goals in a confident and energetic way to keep people enthused and to keep spirits up. When it comes to turning the goals into action, then my colleagues are completely empowered. It is not for me to interfere other than to monitor progress or to deal with a breakdown of trust. But fortunately that is rare.

These issues are examined in detail later in the book. The formulation of direction, goals and values of the firm and the team, and the part that professionals and support people can play in this process, is covered in Chapter 4. Communications are dealt with in Chapter 5. The empowerment of individuals, literally the giving away of power by the team leader to the team members, is considered from various perspectives in Chapters 4, 5, 6, 7 and 8.

BUILD TRUST

The essence of the relationship between professionals and their clients is one of integrity and trust. Whenever I ask professionals and their support colleagues what they expect of their team leaders it is no surprise to me to find that they express similar sentiments. They want to be able to trust their team leaders' motives. They will accept influence and guidance if they believe that team leaders see their prime task as one of helping others rather than purely themselves. They expect their team leaders to be open and honest. They expect them to do what they promise. They judge them by their actions rather than by their words. They expect team leaders to live consistently by the values that the firm and they themselves advocate. Above all they expect team leaders to listen. They expect them really to listen and to take account whenever possible of their ideas, opinions and concerns, and when it is not possible they expect to receive a clear explanation. This is integrity and trust in practice. Values are explored further in Chapter 4 and there is more on listening in Chapter 5.

WORK ON THE LEADERSHIP SPECIFICS

In the box 'Leadership activities and behaviour', there is a list of activities and ways of behaving commonly associated with the leadership role. It is not an exhaustive list and nor is every factor necessarily relevant to leaders of all professional teams. However, it is quite likely that you do, or are expected to, undertake quite a few of the activities, use many of the skills and engage in a number of the behaviours described.

LEADERSHIP ACTIVITIES AND BEHAVIOUR

General leadership skills

▌ Leads by example.

▌ Ensures that team decisions are converted into action.

❙ Expects high standards to be met.

❙ Encourages others to be productive and provide high-quality service.

❙ Acknowledges and gives recognition for good performance.

❙ Creates a climate of energy and enthusiasm.

❙ Clearly explains desired results.

❙ Makes sure team members have the resources to accomplish tasks.

❙ Monitors progress on assignments.

❙ Lets people know when performance is not up to requirements.

❙ Helps team members to improve by giving feedback constructively and sensitively.

❙ Coaches team members to help them to learn, improve and adapt.

❙ Encourages team members to attend appropriate training programmes.

❙ Gives challenging assignments to competent team members.

❙ Ensures that the team has clearly defined objectives and action plans.

❙ Involves team members in the setting of team objectives and action plans.

❙ Encourages team members to support and work in accordance with the firm's objectives and strategy.

❙ Encourages team members to support and work in accordance with the team's objectives and strategy.

❙ Stimulates creativity in others.

■ Fosters good teamwork by encouraging mutual support and help with skill development.

■ Enforces standards in a prompt and sensitive manner.

■ Uses the work scheduling process to aid skill development among team members.

Relationships

■ Treats individuals fairly.

■ Considers the feelings of others when giving opinions.

■ Maintains cooperative working relationships with colleagues inside and outside the team.

■ Cares about the feelings of others.

■ Doesn't try to force opinions on others.

■ Helps others to think things through.

■ Makes others feel comfortable.

■ Builds trust among colleagues.

■ Shows awareness of the needs of others.

Dealing with conflicts

■ Mediates effectively when there are conflicts between individuals.

■ Willing to take an unpopular stand when necessary.

■ Resolves conflicting demands among team members.

■ Avoids compromising too quickly.

■ Looks for creative solutions to conflicts whereby each person's interests are broadly satisfied.

■ When involved in disagreements works towards the best solution rather than trying to win.

Communications skills

■ Keeps team members informed of impending changes.

■ Keeps others who will be affected informed about personal plans and activities.

■ Keeps team members informed about the firm's performance.

■ Keeps team members informed about the team's performance.

■ Listens willingly to the concerns of others.

■ Listens willingly to disagreements from team members.

■ Listens to others without interrupting.

■ Fosters a climate where others are free to air feelings.

■ Speaks effectively in front of a group.

■ Is persuasive orally.

■ Is good at communicating through effective questioning.

■ Gets points across well when talking.

■ Writes clear and concise business documents.

■ Ensures that team members understand the firm's objectives and strategy.

■ Ensures that team members understand the team's objectives and strategy.

▮ Runs good meetings that are time efficient and at which people contribute enthusiastically.

Planning and organizing work

▮ Makes plans that are clear.

▮ Makes plans that are realistic.

▮ Anticipates problems.

▮ Uses plans to help to manage.

▮ Involves others who are affected in the planning process.

▮ Organizes and schedules tasks effectively.

▮ Coordinates work with other departments.

▮ Deals with higher-priority tasks first.

▮ Establishes effective procedures for getting work done.

▮ Makes good use of own time.

▮ Processes paperwork quickly.

▮ Returns phone calls and deals with requests promptly.

▮ Keeps information and documents in an orderly manner.

▮ Sets personal goals daily and achieves them.

▮ Handles details without getting bogged down.

Making decisions

▮ Involves the team in making key professional and business decisions.

■ Gets good relevant information before deciding.

■ Considers options thoroughly before deciding what to do.

■ Avoids making rash decisions.

■ Makes decisions on time.

■ Acts decisively when required.

■ Learns from the results of previous decisions.

Personal attributes

■ Accepts responsibility for own mistakes.

■ Deals with pressure constructively.

■ Deploys confidence in difficult situations.

■ Deals with ambiguity constructively.

■ Responds openly to the ideas of others.

■ Persists at tasks despite unexpected difficulties.

■ Displays a high level of energy and enthusiasm.

■ Keeps up to date with developments related to own work.

■ Sought by others for professional, technical and business knowledge.

■ Knowledgeable about people and operations of the team and the firm as a whole.

■ Can be depended on to get the job done.

You might find it useful to check yourself against the list. Which ones do you regard as being relevant to your role? Which ones are you good at? Do you think that your team members would agree with your analysis? Do you think that it would be helpful to get some informal feedback from them? Just as we learn about our effectiveness in providing services by seeking feedback in one way or another from our clients, so we can also learn about our competence as leaders by seeking feedback from our team members. (See Chapters 1,6 and 7 for thoughts on giving and receiving sensitive and constructive feedback.)

In addition to the activities and ways of behaving listed in the box, you are quite likely to have a number of other leadership responsibilities. The exact ones will depend on the policies and culture of the firm in which you work but are likely to include selection and induction of new recruits; performance review or appraisal; measurement of team and individual performance; scheduling assignments; obtaining feedback from clients; monitoring profitability of assignments; representing your team elsewhere in the firm; and managing specific projects. Clearly the time available for leadership and management activities will always be limited by the need to remain at the coalface and undertake some technical or professional work personally. The chances are it is not going to be possible for you to do all of the things listed in the box and mentioned elsewhere in the text. There is a need to do some prioritizing. Which activities are you expected to undertake by your firm or by your boss? Indeed, are there any clear expectations? If not, perhaps it would be a good idea to check out with those concerned. Which activities do your team members expect or desire you to perform? Which activities do you believe would be most likely to raise the performance of your team? It is a very useful exercise, if it is not provided for already, to write down the roles, responsibilities and performance standards for your leadership work. As a leader of professionals you are likely to have limited power and authority by virtue of your position alone. You are probably perceived as 'first among equals'. To attempt to impose your will on your team is a recipe for disaster. You need to gain the agreement of your colleagues as to the extent and nature of your leadership roles and responsibilities.

ACCEPT PEOPLE'S DIFFERENCES

Have you ever stopped to think about the very different ways that people tackle their assignments and relate to their clients and colleagues? If so, then you have probably noticed that some people seem to wear their personalities on their sleeves and others keep their real concerns to themselves. With some people, what you see is what you get. With others, it takes time and trust for them to open up. You may have noticed that when it comes to communications some people just want the broad picture whilst others prefer chapter and verse. Those who want the broad picture are irritated with a detailed report full of appendices and statistical analyses. Those who prefer details are usually uncomfortable with having a broad outline only. You may have observed that some people make their decisions in a completely impersonal way. Emphasis is placed on fairness and equity. Justice is the order of the day. Others find it almost impossible to take decisions without considering the personal dimensions. Sentiment may be valued above logic. If forced to choose between tact and truth, tact may win the day. Some people keep detailed 'to do' lists, know exactly what they are going to do for the month ahead and even plan their holidays a year in advance. To others, these ways of behaving are a complete anathema. Adaptability and spontaneity are the characteristics that appeal.

Some of us think that people are uninterested or withholding information in a meeting when in fact they are working things out in their heads. Others have the impression that someone is uncertain or inconsistent when that person is thinking aloud. Some people fall into the trap of believing that others are unimaginative when in fact they are raising realistic and practical questions. Some of us make the mistake of thinking that our colleagues are procrastinating and unreliable when they are trying to keep options open. Some people see others as rigid and controlling when they are in fact preparing careful plans and schedules. Sometimes our judgements of other people are biased as a result of our own ways of seeing things and making decisions. Some of us even go so far as to fall into the trap of believing that everybody else sees the world in the same way that we do.

Team leaders who take people's differences and the root causes of their own preferences into account find it easier to communicate and develop a good rapport with their colleagues. It is useful to have some guidelines to help us to understand these differences in a straightforward and relatively simple way. A good starting point is the work of the Swiss psychiatrist Carl Jung and the mother-and-daughter partnership of Katherine Briggs and Isabel Briggs Myers. Jung's 1923 work *Psychological Types* provides the basic personality classifications. Myers and Briggs subsequently designed a psychological instrument that explains differences according to Jung's theory of personality preferences.

The Myers Briggs Type Indicator is one of the most widely used psycho-metric tests of preferences. It is used throughout the world and has been translated into many languages. An effective way for leaders and their teams to understand differences and the implications for communications, relationships, ways of working and so on is to complete the Myers Briggs Type Indicator (MBTI) and to reflect on the results. Many businesses and other organizations, especially those that take leadership development and teamwork seriously, arrange for this to happen.

Abbott Mead Vickers is a high-performing advertising agency. It is also a good place to work. It was ranked in the 2001, 2002 and 2003 *Sunday Times* Best Companies to Work For league tables. Myers Briggs is used extensively as part of its leadership and team development programme. Development Director Alison Chadwick explains the benefits:

> Although most of our people tend to have good self-awareness and understanding of others (these are important hiring criteria after all) we find that Myers Briggs gives an extra dimension. It is robust but easy to understand and the insights it provides help people build and maintain productive and harmonious relationships both internally and with clients. It helps our leaders manage diversity and gives them insights into how they can beneficially adapt their styles to the preferences of others. This is especially valuable for teamwork. With an understanding of Myers Briggs it is easier for team members to welcome and work constructively with differences between them, and to gain more cohesion as a team. Another benefit of Myers Briggs is the perspective it can give people on how they react to stress. Advertising is a challenging business, and insights that help people manage stress are always valuable.

A simple description of basic differences follows. It is based on the work of Jung, Myers and Briggs. It provides a starting point for understanding how different people tick and how they like to be treated. Readers who are not familiar with the Myers Briggs Type Indicator may feel that it would be useful, subsequently, for them and their teams to complete it and to discuss the implications with a qualified adviser.

Four factors that influence the ways in which people behave are considered:

▌ how people prefer to relate to others;

▌ how people prefer to gather and use information;

▌ how people prefer to make decisions;

▌ how people prefer to organize themselves and their work.

People have to relate every day with clients and their colleagues. Some people prefer to do this in an extraverted way, meeting frequently with others, talking through ideas, taking initiatives in relationships and being sociable and expressive. Other people are rather more introverted, preferring to think things through by themselves before talking with others. Sometimes they prefer to communicate in writing. They often wish to be private and contained.

When gathering and using information some people are more comfortable with facts, details and practical applications. They trust experience and they like to work with ideas that have been tested. Others are happier with the big picture. They tend to look for future opportunities. They enjoy ideas and looking at patterns and meanings in data, and they trust inspiration.

When making decisions, some people are very analytical, use cause-and-effect reasoning, strive for objectivity and solve problems with logic. They sometimes appear to be tough minded. They like people to be treated equitably and with justice. Others tend to make decisions primarily in keeping with their values and beliefs. They like to consider what is important to them and to the others involved. They may appear to be tender minded. They like people to be treated from an individual perspective. They are empathetic.

Finally, some people prefer to behave in a planned and orderly way, seeking to regulate and manage their lives. They like to resolve issues quickly and move on. They make plans, short and long term, and are methodical and systematic. Others prefer to live in a flexible, spontaneous way, seeking to experience and understand life rather than to control it. They like to collect as much information as possible before arriving at decisions. They like to adapt to last-minute options. They often feel energized by 11th-hour pressures. These differences are summed up in Figure 2.1.

Here are some tips for working constructively with your team members by taking individual differences into account:

▌ **Working with extraverts:**
  – Let extraverts speak their minds without always holding them to what they say.
  – Communicate face to face whenever possible.

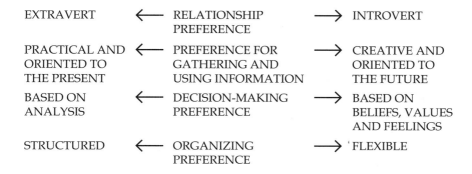

Figure 2.1 Personality differences

- Give them plenty of opportunities to express, to talk and to share.
- Provide plenty of positive feedback.
- Be tolerant when they think aloud.

▌ **Working with introverts:**
- Give them time to reflect.
- Follow up important conversations in writing whenever possible.
- 'Open the door' for them in meetings by specifically inviting them to contribute or asking if they wish to comment.
- Provide peace and quiet for concentration.
- Be tolerant when they need time to think before responding.

▌ **Working with those who have a practical preference when gathering and using information:**
- Provide information in a step-by-step fashion with lots of facts and examples.
- Dot Is and cross Ts.
- Focus on rules, deadlines, traditions and rituals.
- Give specific answers.
- Concentrate on the immediate and short-term issues and benefits.
- Be literal.

▌ **Working with those who have a creative preference when gathering and using information:**
- Give them plenty of opportunities to contribute their own ideas.
- Focus on reason and principles.
- Use insights and imagination to provoke discussion.

- Don't worry about not being literal.
- Concentrate on the longer-term issues and benefits.
- Harness their problem-solving capabilities.

▌ **Working with those who have a preference for bringing analysis to the decision-making process:**
- Give them plenty of opportunities to analyse data.
- Give them a chance to challenge ideas.
- Appeal to their sense of fairness, justice and equity.
- Use cause-and-effect and pros-and-cons analyses with them when assessing options.

▌ **Working with those who have a preference for bringing personal values and beliefs to the decision-making process:**
- Allow for their values when they are seeking to understand and decide.
- Recognize their strong concern for harmony and support among colleagues.
- Provide lots of positive feedback.
- Emphasize the benefits to people of proposals that you make.

▌ **Working with those who prefer a structured approach to life:**
- Provide agendas, schedules and plans.
- Give plenty of advance warning of changes.
- Try to avoid too many surprises.
- Don't leave issues open for too long.

▌ **Working with those who prefer a flexible approach to life:**
- Provide plenty of room for manoeuvre.
- Recognize that they have a strong need to determine matters for themselves.
- Leave things open as long as possible.
- Provide scope, where possible, for a flexible approach to assignments and projects.

Clearly none of us should follow these suggestions in a slave-like fashion. There will be many occasions when the nature of tasks and the requirements of the firm in which we work prevent us from behaving in these ways. However, they are useful tips to bear in mind and to apply in a balanced way when circumstances permit.

BE AWARE AND ALLOW
FOR YOUR OWN PREFERENCES

If you know your own preferences then you will understand yourself better and that is likely to enhance your relationships with others. Also, if you know your own preferences you will be more aware of your own biases and that will help you to avoid stereotyping others in a negative fashion.

A very helpful thing for us all to do is to develop the capacity to think and behave, at least to some degree, in opposite ways to our preferences. This helps us to be more versatile. It also helps us to become more aware and sensitive to those who are different. It helps us to be more empathetic by allowing us to stand in their shoes and see the world from their perspective.

Here are a few simple ways of doing this:

- *If you are an extravert.*   Your tendency is to speak first and listen second. Force yourself to listen more. Occasionally in meetings sit back and say nothing. Reflect back what other people have said before offering a reply.

- *If you are an introvert.*   Your tendency is to reflect and contemplate. Try some small talk by gossiping over coffee or before your meeting starts. Speak up in meetings, early on, without being asked.

- *If you are practical.*   Your tendency is to stay attentive to current issues. Give reign to your imagination. Give yourself a target to come up with one new idea per day about work, leisure, family and so on for a month.

- *If you are creative.*   Your tendency is to think about possibilities and the future. Concentrate on the present and forget the future for a while. Enjoy what is going on around you. Give some information to a colleague in a literal step-by-step fashion.

- *If you are analytical.*   Your tendency is to be objective and impersonal. Next time you make a decision appeal to the heart as well as to the head. Think about the implications of the decision for other people.

- *If you are a 'feeling' person.*   Your tendency is to want harmony and to base decisions on beliefs and values. When disagreement occurs in a meeting, avoid rescuing others. Say to yourself, 'It is only an exchange of ideas; there is nothing personal'. Try your hand at reaching a decision between options based entirely on a pros-and-cons analysis.

▌ *If you are structured.*   Your tendency is to want a planned and scheduled existence. Try to let things happen. Occasionally let one thing that bothers you go unattended.

▌ *If you are flexible.*   Your tendency is to be spontaneous and to keep options open. Try to finish some important tasks ahead of schedule and promise yourself that you won't be distracted until the jobs are done.

ADAPT LEADERSHIP STYLE TO DIFFERENT SITUATIONS

Many successful team leaders find it helpful to vary their styles by reference to the situation that they find themselves in. Hersey and Blanchard (1993) have developed a useful framework. The idea is for leaders to vary the amount of personal encouragement, support and recognition (relationship behaviour) and the amount of direction and structure (task behaviour) according to the nature of the work that people do and their ability and willingness to undertake their tasks. Ability is a function of knowledge, skills and experience, and willingness is a combination of motivation to achieve and personal confidence. An adaptation of Hersey and Blanchard's framework is illustrated in Figure 2.2.

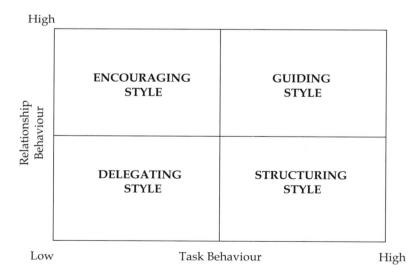

Figure 2.2   Leadership styles

The leader using the structuring style decides how the task should be carried out and then tells the team member what to do, how to do it and with whom, when and where. Frequent and regular monitoring of performance occurs and there is prompt reinforcement of good work. The style is most effective when there is a clear desire to help the person concerned to do a good job. This is a very hands-on leadership style and is likely to be necessary only rarely in a professional service context. If someone is undertaking a task for the first time and lacks confidence or feels insecure then there is a case for using it in a very sensitive, warm and friendly manner.

The leader using the guiding style explains why and how the task needs to be undertaken and agrees appropriate targets and performance standards. Some help with the development of knowledge and skills is usual. Discussions are held regularly and frequently. Performance feedback is given and further assistance with the development of abilities is provided. There is an emphasis on learning whilst doing. The guiding style is very useful in a professional service environment when someone is motivated and confident and brings to the task some relevant knowledge and skill but still needs to learn more in order to do a first-class job. It is particularly appropriate with trainees.

The leader using the encouraging style does so to help the team member to increase self-confidence and ability to perform the task outstandingly well and independently. The encouraging style involves lots of discussion about the task and a sharing of views on how it should be tackled. The person performing the task is encouraged to specify his or her own performance standards or targets. Progress is reviewed jointly with emphasis placed on building self-confidence so that the task can be undertaken independently in the future. The encouraging style is particularly useful with able young professionals who are not yet fully experienced and who are not yet quite ready to work alone.

The last of the four styles involves delegating the decision making and the planning that relate to the task, as well as the implementation. The leader, using the delegation style, allows the team member to operate independently. There is no, or only occasional, monitoring of performance. The team leader provides support and help if it is requested. The initiative to seek help is left primarily to the person doing the work. The delegating style is ideal when the person has the knowledge, skill and experience to do an outstanding job and is self-confident and highly motivated. It is leading with a light touch. Generally speaking, those professionals who are technically very competent, self-assured and highly motivated react very well. It is important, however, for team leaders to beware of using it when people are not ready. The risks for the firm and for the individual are clearly considerable.

Most of us can see the logic of adapting our styles to meet the needs of the situations in which we find ourselves. In practice, however, we often lead in a way that suits us or in a way that we find comfortable. Some of us find it difficult, for instance, to 'let go' or relinquish control and may fail to use the delegating style when it should be used. Others find it awkward to be warm and give support. Thus the encouraging style becomes difficult to use. Some people resent the time that the guiding style involves and so fail to use it when it is needed. Some of us shrink from the structuring style, especially in a professional environment, because we fear that we may be seen as patronizing.

There are two final points. First, it is helpful for leaders to discuss, with their team members, the need to use one style rather than another. It is often the case that different styles are needed for different tasks or assignments. Easy, open communications about these matters are helpful. It is all part of the process of fostering trust. It is a good thing for team leaders to talk freely with their colleagues about the best style to use in particular circumstances. The second point is to bear in mind the old adage, 'We judge ourselves by our intentions and others judge us by our actions'. We may believe that we are using the right style for the right situation but others may regard our leadership behaviour as different from what we intend. Again, frank communications are important. The likelihood of misperception is reduced if we talk openly about the appropriateness of using one style rather than another with particular individuals for specific tasks.

3

Devoting the time and energy to lead successfully

I am a leader by default,
only because nature does not allow a vacuum.

— (Archbishop Desmond Tutu)

It is far from being a universal problem but many leaders of teams of professionals are reluctant to devote enough time and attention to the responsibilities involved. According to John Stapleton, Managing Partner of Thomas Eggar, a large law firm in the South of England, there are two reasons:

> Many of our people became lawyers because that was the work that they wanted to do and that's what they were trained for. They didn't join us because they had a passion to be leaders or managers. In this sense they are very different from graduates who join large corporations as management trainees. Young people who become management trainees do so presumably because they have an ambition to run a bit of the organization or, maybe, eventually take charge of the whole thing. Similarly,

> graduates who join the army and go to Sandhurst are trained specifically to be leaders. That's the whole point.
>
> When we appoint people as team leaders they are sometimes reluctant to devote enough time to the task because the work involved will take them away, to some extent, from the thing that they enjoy doing most, which is the legal work for the clients. They don't want to let go of the seam of gold – the client base.
>
> Secondly, there is the fear factor. People worry that if they give up too much of their fee-earning work then they will get out of touch. They become concerned that if later on they were to give up the leadership job then they would find it difficult to get back to being an effective full-time lawyer.

I have come across similar sentiments in other professional activities such as consultancy, software development, education, accountancy, scientific work, engineering and design. They occur in professional service firms but also among professionals working within large corporations and elsewhere.

In quite a few small and medium-sized professional service firms there is another factor that contributes to reluctance. Even though there may be protestations to the contrary from the top, many members of the firm believe that the bigger financial rewards accrue to those who personally generate the higher fees. Leadership of teams is regarded therefore as an undervalued activity. In some cases the problem is exacerbated by the fact that the only overt individual performance measurement that is used is whether or not fee-earning targets are achieved. It is a classic case of the old business maxim, 'What gets measured gets done'.

There is one more associated problem. Even when the importance of the leadership function is fully acknowledged, some leaders of professionals find it hard to delegate work. The more common reasons are:

▊ They believe that nobody else can do the work as well as they can.

▊ They reserve tasks for themselves because they enjoy them or they like the recognition that they receive from their clients.

▊ They believe that they have insufficient time to explain the tasks or coach others to do them.

▊ They fear that others will make mistakes and that the consequences will be disastrous. (This is especially true in the risk-averse professions such as law and accountancy.)

▌ They lack confidence in the abilities of their team members.

Schooling ourselves to be willing and able to delegate is a prerequisite. It helps, also, to seek the following:

▌ an agreement with seniors to have sufficient time to do the leadership job;

▌ an agreement that financial rewards will be based, at least in part, on leadership performance;

▌ a commitment from senior management to extol the importance of the team leadership function.

CREATE THE TIME
TO DO THE LEADERSHIP JOB

Sometimes for senior leaders the job is full time. For managing partners in a large firm that is a sensible idea. However, I believe strongly that leaders of teams should normally continue to undertake work directly for clients. Leadership by example in professional work cannot be over-estimated. To be able to demonstrate good practice provides credibility. Actions speak louder than words. It is much easier for people to coach others if they are known to be successfully doing professional work themselves. The important thing is to achieve a sensible balance between leadership activities, on the one hand, and all of the other activities that have to be undertaken on the other.

The national law firm DLA has evolved a useful way of dealing with this issue. Robert Halton, the Human Resources Director, persuaded the firm to reject the distinction of 'fee-earning' and 'non-fee-earning' time. (This difference is still commonly observed, especially in accountancy and

---

FIRM'S TIME AT DLA

The partners were invited to indicate how many hours they spent, on average, working for the firm each year. They arrived at a total of 2,300 hours. They took into account the average number of hours spent working each week and deducted time for holidays. Each partner now agrees an allocation of hours for each year as part of the performance management process. The allocations vary depending on the precise nature of the job but typically are as follows:

Leadership and team management	350
Strategic planning and budgeting	50
Business development and marketing	350
Financial management	100
Personal development	100
Wider partnership role	50
Professional work	1,300

The total for each person adds up to 2,300

law firms.) He introduced the notion of firm's time instead. In the box 'Firm's time at DLA', you can see how it works.

A similar exercise is undertaken for associates and solicitors. Not everyone, of course, has leadership responsibilities so that category does not always apply. However, all lawyers now think in terms of total time and how it should be subdivided between different activities for them, rather than 'fee-earning' and 'non-fee-earning' time.

Robert Halton has this to say about the benefits:

Language is important. It reflects what people think. We used to talk in terms of professional and non-professional staff and fee earners and non-fee earners. That is not good news as far as teamwork is concerned.

Likewise we used to talk about chargeable hours and non-chargeable hours. It was as if the only thing that lawyers did that was important was the fee earning. Of course the fee earning is critically important but so is how people use the rest of their time. We now talk about clients' time. That is doing the technical work for the clients and meeting with them. We also talk about firm's time or investment time. It includes marketing activities, personal development and contributing to the part-nership generally. The notion is underscored by all of the lawyers having a target number of hours for these activities, in addition to their targets for professional work. As far as team leaders are concerned it includes target time, of course, for leadership work.

Total contribution is now part of the remuneration system. Rewarding people for being successful in the investment activities reinforces their behaviour. Clearly, people are more likely to go on doing these things well if there is a pay-off. It has taken time but this new way of thinking is now bedding down in the culture. We are not completely there yet but we are well on our way. The benefits are clear. Increasingly our people are business people as well as being professional people.

If you work in an organization where the notion of agreeing time to perform the leadership function is well established, then that is fine. If not, then why not seek an agreement on this issue as a matter of priority with your senior colleagues?

REWARD LEADERSHIP PERFORMANCE

Leaders of professionals are more likely to give the right amount of time to do the job if the financial rewards are based on the performance of their teams rather than on their own individual professional or technical competence. The old adage, 'Tell me how I am going to be rewarded and I will tell you how I am going to behave' is pertinent. The way to encourage devotion to leadership tasks is, in part, to reward people for the successful outcome of those tasks.

It is relatively easy to reward leaders of professionals in a way that reflects the performance of their teams if the service is being provided to colleagues in, say, a large corporation. It is also fairly easy in those professional service firms where individual fee earning is not glorified at the expense of all else. There is a much greater problem for firms, still quite often found in the law and accountancy sectors, where individual fee earning is valued as the only truly worthwhile activity. In such firms there is often deep suspicion of, and irritation with, anyone who, for whatever reason, is not required personally to generate a 'full load' of fees. Indeed, individual fee earning is in a sense regarded as a virility symbol. Individuals prove their worth in one way only, through the generation of fees. For these firms, switching to rewarding leaders for team rather than individual performance is not easy. However, if they want team leadership to be valued and for leaders to give sufficient time to the work involved then this is probably the single most important step that they can take. Doubters among accountants and lawyers might reflect on one simple fact. They know that first-class leadership is a key determinant of success in their clients' firms. Why do they think that it should be any different for their own businesses?

John Stapleton, Managing Partner of law firm Thomas Eggar, has this to say:

> We now have team targets and we measure the team leaders' performance on the basis of their teams' successes rather than for their individual professional work. We believe that more value is added to the firm when teams are well led. In other words, we are not paying lip service to the importance of leadership. Our belief in it is enshrined in good hard measures and rewards.

If you work in an organization where your competence as a team leader, in addition to your performance as a professional and technical contributor, is rewarded, then so well and good. If not, why not argue the case for it to be done?

EXTOL THE LEADERSHIP FUNCTION

Professionals are more likely to devote the right amount of time and energy to the leadership job if it is clearly valued. In your firm, is there a belief, widely shared, that good leadership helps to produce first-class results? Is this notion rooted deeply in the culture of the organization? If the answers to these questions are yes, then it is likely that some, at least, of the following activities are taking place:

▌ Senior people, for instance managing partners and partnership board members, behave as effective leaders. They lead by example and become role models.

▌ Senior people communicate the message that high-performing teams, well motivated, inspired and coached by good leaders, contribute to success for the firm and for everyone's careers. The message is communicated both one to one and in groups. It is put across orally and in writing. It is repeated regularly and in novel ways.

▌ People who lead effectively are rewarded and recognized specifically for doing just that.

▌ The firm makes it clear that the criteria for promotion to partner include evidence of leadership skills, as well as professional competence and an ability to win business.

▌ Significant resources are devoted to leadership training and development as well as specific professional and technical training.

▌ Senior people act as cheerleaders. They communicate good leadership and teamwork practice that they notice in one part of the firm to teams elsewhere in the organization.

John Stapleton, Managing Partner of Thomas Eggar, puts it this way:

> We now talk about being leaders before lawyers. Our equity partners are lawyers, of course, but our role as lawyers is subsidiary to our role as leaders within a law firm. For the business to prosper it has to be run properly and be competitive with other legal firms. To be competitive, the business needs the equity partners, the owners, to be fully functioning leaders – leaders of teams, leaders of departments and leaders of geographical locations. We all need to lead members of our teams in the same direction. The firm agrees the direction. Our equity partners, our leaders, increasingly share a common strategic vision. We are becoming more entrepreneurial and we are becoming better at leading by example.

If the importance of good leadership is heralded in your firm, then that is good news. If it isn't, then why not try to influence senior people towards the value of proclaiming the virtues of good leadership by their own actions and words of mouth? See Chapter 14 for some ideas on improving influencing skills.

DEVELOP BOTH A WILLINGNESS AND THE SKILLS TO DELEGATE

Here are some simple tips for overcoming a reluctance to delegate:

▌ You may have a desire for perfection and feel that you are the only person who can do the work. If so, start by delegating parts of the tasks concerned and coach people to perform them to your satisfaction.

▌ You may reserve tasks for yourself because you enjoy doing them or you enjoy the recognition that you get from your clients. If so, try to achieve satisfaction from other parts of your job instead, for example undertaking the leadership function including coaching, running effective team sessions and involving people in business planning.

▌ You may feel that you have insufficient time to explain tasks or coach others to do them. If so, reflect on the fact that the time spent helping others to perform tasks effectively now will save you time and effort in the longer run. By coaching others now, you are investing in their competence.

▌ You may fear failure because others will make mistakes and that the consequences will be disastrous. Identify possible risks with individuals and help them to develop their skills. Good leaders take risks to help people grow and develop. However, minimize the risks by coaching well and working with your people before they fly solo.

▌ You may lack confidence in the abilities of your team members. If so, carefully assess what individuals can and cannot do. Then delegate the tasks that you are confident can be tackled and on a gradual basis coach people to undertake the others

It is evident that the more effective a professional team leader is at coaching, the more comfortable he or she will be with the process of delegating. The two things go hand in hand. Obvious though this is, it is surprising how often good coaching is neglected in practice. The skills involved in being an effective coach are explored in some detail in Chapter 7.

USE YOUR TIME EFFECTIVELY

Leaders of professional service teams are very busy people. Juggling the pressures of the leadership function with the professional work, client relations and marketing and selling activities is far from easy. If you find it difficult to manage your time effectively you can do no better than think about, and try out, the very practical tips offered by Martin Scott, an expert in time management, in his book of that name (1992). The ideas that follow draw on his work:

▌ Think clearly about problems and symptoms. If you lack time then it is probably due to your having unclear objectives, prioritizing poorly and planning ineffectively. Clear objectives, good and careful prioritizing and planning are the keys to using time effectively.

■ For team leaders in particular, the concept of leverage is important. Assess what makes a difference in the long run in your work. What are the tasks requiring investment of time and effort now that will actually save you time in the longer run? Make sure that you spend a reasonable amount of time on these 'high-leverage' tasks each week.

'High-leverage' tasks, which are investments of time to save time in the future, include setting clear objectives, planning future work, developing systems and building and maintaining relationships with people who can help you to succeed in your work. They include coaching your people so that you can delegate more work to them and gaining commitment from your team members to high levels of performance. Reading, talking to others and attending training courses, thereby developing your own abilities, are also examples of high-leverage tasks.

Remember Pareto's Law: 'Most people get 80 per cent of their results from 20 per cent of their effort and 20 per cent of their results from 80 per cent of their effort.' Good use of leverage could allow you to get a much better return from your work.

■ Try to minimize distractions from high-leverage and other important tasks. The main distractions are when we:
  - spend most of our time coping with urgencies, crises and panics, leaving no time for high-leverage and other important tasks, with the result that we go on being overwhelmed by urgencies, crises and panics in the limited time available;
  - enjoy fire-fighting: it is much more fun to solve crises than doing the slow, boring, tedious but necessary tasks of setting objectives and planning;
  - do comfortable, easy tasks rather than important ones;
  - do and tick off the quick and easy tasks on our lists of work to be done to provide the immediate gratification of having accomplished something;
  - allow the post-adrenalin dip, following a high that comes from pulling off new business, completing a successful negotiation or achieving a breakthrough, to continue for too long;
  - allow team members to delegate their problems upwards to us rather than helping them to solve and deal with the problems for themselves.

Avoid distractions from high-leverage and other important tasks by allocating regular amounts of time to tackle them. Do routine and less important tasks faster (like the day before your last holiday when you cleared your desk in double-quick time).

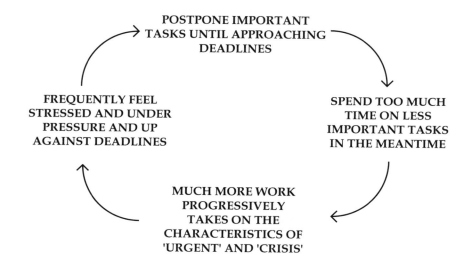

Figure 3.1   Vicious circle

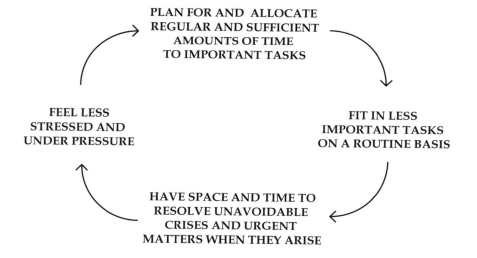

Figure 3.2   Virtuous circle

Effective team leaders are ruthless about their priorities. One way to cope is to list all of the tasks that you need to do tomorrow. Then rewrite them in order of importance. Work through them. The last task tomorrow is to list the next day's activities and priorities. It won't work perfectly but it will begin to shift the balance of work from the urgent to the important.

Avoid the vicious circle of behaviour shown in Figure 3.1 by following the virtuous circle of behaviour shown in Figure 3.2.

▍ Avoid procrastination. Here are the more common reasons why people procrastinate at work, together with some simple solutions:

- The task is so big you don't know where to start. The answer is to break the job down into small chunks. If you are writing a report, for instance, plan the structure, gather the data, write the draft, refine and finish.
- The task involves making difficult decisions. You don't know what to do. The best way to overcome this problem is to follow a simple procedure: 1) Ascertain the deadline for the decision. 2) Collect information. 3) List options. 4) Evaluate options by listing pros and cons. 5) Check tentative decision with others. 6) Decide. 7) Treat the matter as closed. Don't agonize over decisions taken. Remember you will always get some wrong but most will probably be right.
- The task involves doing something unpleasant like discussing poor performance with a team member or admitting a mistake to a client. A simple solution is to mentally list the advantages and disadvantages of postponing the decision. In 99 times out of 100 the answer is obvious, that is to take early action.
- You are feeling low. A good way to resolve this is to take some exercise or get some fresh air. Another possibility is to tackle a tiresome but quick job even if it is not of high priority. Getting it out of the way gives a lift.
- You have trouble getting started. Why not cut off the 'escape routes'? For example, always have a clear desk and close the door or find a quiet place for concentrated effort. Discipline yourself to do real work within a few minutes of arriving at the office.
- You have trouble finishing a project. One answer is to break the task down into sub-tasks and reward yourself before moving on. For instance, you could take a coffee, have a chat or look at the newspaper for five minutes (but not before the sub-task has been completed).

▍ Keep your desk tidy. A cluttered desk is not a sign of genius despite what those with impossibly untidy desks will tell you. It gives rise to two major time wasters: searching for papers, reports, notes and letters; and periodic spring-cleaning, ie sorting, tidying and filing.

The solution is simple. When paper arrives on your desk, ask the question, 'Am I ever going to do anything with this?' If the answer is no, then chuck it out. Don't be scared, because it always gets thrown out when you spring-clean. If the answer is yes, then ask the question 'Can I do it now?' If the answer is yes, because it is a five-minute job, then do it. If the answer is no, put the document in the pending file. Remember that paper placed in a pile will naturally gravitate towards the bottom. An item on a list will automatically rise to the top. Keep lists and avoid piles of paper. The simple trick is to organize the working area rather than to keep tidying it.

▌ Don't be intimidated by, or addicted to reading, e-mails.
- If you have an e-mail alert signal on your computer screen then why not switch it off? Decide how often to check e-mails, for example two or three times per day, but depending on the nature of your work, and stick to your decision.
- Audit your e-mails for the last two weeks. Sort them into the following categories: those that you ignored; those that you actioned immediately; those that you actioned later; and those that you passed to someone else for action.
- Learn from your audit and from then on: delete 'ignore' e-mails immediately; deal with 'action immediately' e-mails at once; put 'action later' e-mails in a folder and deal with all of them at the end of the day; and immediately send 'pass on to someone else for action' e-mails to appropriate recipients.

▌ Avoid being interrupted when engaged in high-concentration tasks. Most professionals have many of these. Let your colleagues know, even if normally it is your policy to be available, that for the next two hours you are writing a paper, doing some research, preparing a design or engaged in some other high-concentration activity and cannot be interrupted. Arrange for colleagues to intercept enquiries both personal and by telephone. Don't abuse the privilege. Keep it short, probably no more than two hours at a time. Let people know that you will be available afterwards and always honour that commitment. Tell them the time that you will be free. Respond immediately to enquiries that you have missed in the meantime. You have to strike the right balance between being available and giving yourself time for concentrated effort. Finally, play the game and be prepared to intercept enquiries for colleagues when they also need uninterrupted time to think, write, design or calculate.

Part Two

Leading professionals – the keys to success

4

Direction: Objectives, values, strategy and change

Where there is no vision, the people perish.
— (Proverbs 29: 18)

*Do not quench your inspiration and imagination;
do not become the slave of your model.*
— (Vincent Van Gogh)

Good leadership is about making things happen. The starting point is for you to help your team to develop a clear sense of direction together with a few important objectives and a strategy for achieving them. It is also helpful to gain agreement on the values that will underpin the ways in which team members will tackle their jobs and the nature of their relationships with clients and colleagues. Whatever is decided must be congruent with the mission, objectives, values and strategy of the firm as a whole.

The purpose of engaging your team in this activity is to formulate a number of actions that will give you a competitive advantage by making your team's services more valuable to clients than those of other firms. It will probably also involve identifying new services to promote, new markets to enter and new clients to target. Profitability will be the watchword. If you lead an in-house professional team in a corporation then the purpose is to develop an action plan for providing new and improved services to your internal clients.

Notice the emphasis here on the leader involving the team members in formulating a clear sense of direction. The fashion, these days, is to talk of outstanding leaders providing a captivating vision of the future to which everyone can readily and happily sign up. My experience of working with them is that the best leaders of professionals do not impose their own ideas on their colleagues. Nor do they 'sell' them to their colleagues. Rather they work with them, through a subtle blend of encouragement, helpful questions, thoughtful suggestions and the bringing together of useful ideas to generate a clear and agreed picture of the desirable future for the team. I suspect that this approach is one that not only suits the temperaments of most professionals but also produces the best results.

At DLA the process of business planning involves leaders and their teams at the corporate level on the one hand, and among the practice groups (such as commercial, litigation, real estate and banking), geographical locations and support functions on the other.

Managing Partner Nigel Knowles explains it this way:

> We establish the vision for the firm at corporate level. This involves brainstorming sessions and discussions with members of the DLA board, the practice group heads, the managing partners of the offices and the support function directors. We also have a number of clearly articulated values, covering people, service and quality. At first they were aspirational but increasingly they reflect reality.
>
> We get the practice group heads, regional office partners and support function directors to work out, in close consultation with their team members, strategic plans to achieve the vision, as it applies to their parts of the business. It has to support the firm's values. The process of consultation by the various team leaders is a genuine one of involvement. Team leaders write up draft plans after, not before, thorough brainstorming discussions and agreements among the team members themselves. This is important for ownership and commitment. Draft plans are coordinated by me. My board colleagues, the support function directors and I then prepare a DLA strategy which takes account of the goals and plans prepared by teams throughout the business. We finish up with integrated corporate and unit

plans for achieving our vision over a three-year period and which also support our values. We believe that such a comprehensive planning process is unusual for a law firm. We have now been through this process twice and we are well up the learning curve. We have had to work hard to get people to believe in it.

We encourage relatively short plans with a few significant goals and some well-constructed action points. They must be realistic and deliverable and must be followed up. People inside and outside the business can now see that DLA is focused and has a clear corporate personality. Our business results have been excellent and our progress has been outstanding. Internal cynicism has evaporated and we get grudging admiration from at least some of our competitors. We reckon that we are now the leading UK law firm.

None of this would be possible without having good leadership throughout the business, in our practice groups, in our regional offices, in our support functions and at the corporate level. Our leaders have to be good at getting their teams to contribute their thinking. They have to work towards a consensus. They need to get commitment from everybody. They need, finally, to encourage everyone to stay focused and turn the plans into action. In other words, the team leaders throughout the firm have to make it happen.

PROVIDE STRATEGIC LEADERSHIP

Providing strategic leadership is not a highly complicated process. Essentially it is about making time to create a vision of the desirable but attainable future state of the team's business; identifying crucial conditions for success; making sure that work is not confused with achievements; and setting up development projects and action points to turn the vision into tangible results.

A good way for the team to formulate effective strategies and action plans is to hold a strategy development workshop. The idea is for the team to spend a day or two away from the office, entirely free from interruptions and other distractions, where participants can concentrate their attention exclusively on the critical issues facing the future of their team. A country house hotel is an ideal venue. The purpose of the workshop is for the team, collectively, to address issues of strategic importance to the business. They may be immediate, short or long term in nature. There are other benefits including the development of collective responsibility among the members of the team; improved motivation and team effectiveness; an opportunity for people to say what they genuinely think and believe and for them to learn more about the purpose, objectives and needs of the team as a whole.

The team leader's main task is to manage the process. It is primarily a facilitating role. It involves helping team members to concentrate their attention on key matters; and to encourage them to be creative and analytical, to face up to contentious issues, to speak openly and frankly and to agree responsibilities and timings for post-workshop action. If the workshop is being held for the first time, then it may be helpful to have an experienced outsider to act as an adviser and facilitator.

It is not uncommon for members of professional service teams to attend monthly meetings at which they do little more than give reports on their own responsibilities and the progress of their own tasks. A strategy workshop helps to overcome this weakness by getting all members to become concerned with the future direction of the team's work without letting their own particular professional interests get in the way. When participants are encouraged to come up with their collective vision for success and action plans for achieving it, they often produce ambitious proposals and rigorously thought-through plans. They are generally more committed to translating such plans into action because they see them as part of their own strategy. There is a sense of ownership.

It is not uncommon to find one team member lacking crucial knowledge of another's roles and responsibilities. A workshop provides opportunities to clarify such matters and to get problems out on the table and resolved constructively in the interests of everyone. In an effective team each participant is willing to say his or her piece openly without fear or favour. Perhaps surprisingly, there are many professional service teams where this does not happen. A major contribution that the team leader (or an experienced outsider) can make is to encourage plain speaking and to assist participants to ask questions that go to the heart of a matter. The ideal workshop is one where all participants are able to think and act in the round and be concerned with the future of the team's business as well as contributing their own technical or professional expertise.

A successful strategy workshop is set up with great care. A venue that provides freedom from interruptions and distractions is crucial. Telephone calls and e-mail transmissions should be forbidden during working sessions and restricted to lunch breaks and other free time. When individuals are frequently interrupted by telephone calls and deliveries of faxed materials it is symptomatic of a deeper malaise. If people are unable to lift their heads from important but nevertheless day-to-day matters for 24 or 48 hours then they are unlikely to be taking a proper strategic view.

Team members should ideally arrive in time for dinner on the evening preceding the workshop to allow the scene to be set and to ensure a prompt start next morning with everyone present. It also provides the opportunity for the development of team spirit and to get participants in the right frame of mind. If it can be arranged then two days is a particularly good span for a workshop. It allows for serious discussion and conclusions to be reached. There are risks involved with a workshop lasting for more than two days. It may well run out of steam and finish with an anticlimax.

It is essential that there are positive outcomes. A talk shop that fails to deliver action creates disenchantment and cynicism and leads to poor motivation. The more useful outcomes are a few business development projects and action points with particular team members accountable, personally or as leaders of small teams, to undertake them. Agreed target dates for completion and implementation are important. The process of steering the team to conclusions, based on a broad consensus, is an important task for the team leader (or outside adviser).

In professional service teams useful strategic outcomes from workshops are likely to include:

▌ the development of new professional services;

▌ the exploitation of new market sectors;

▌ the targeting of selected potential clients;

▌ investments in research activities in order to be more valuable to the clients;

▌ improvements to service delivery through the development of new processes and systems for handling assignments and projects;

▌ innovations in recruitment and selection so that the team provides more value to clients by deploying higher-calibre people;

▌ better training and development arrangements to improve technical, professional, client relations, marketing and leadership skills and thereby provide greater value;

▌ investments in productivity improvements to reduce costs.

If periodic attention is not given to these sorts of issues then the team's behaviour is likely to be one of simply responding to short-term pressures from competitors, clients and economic forces. Good strategic management, and therefore effective performance and higher profits, requires a judicious blend of responding to environmental changes and taking initiatives. It involves both adjusting appropriately to external pressures and establishing leadership in the marketplace with well-thought-out innovations.

Strategy formulation is also about developing a strong culture. The ethos, spirit and drive of a firm; the ways that its people behave towards clients and colleagues; its approach to innovation and service quality; and the values and beliefs widely shared are the essence of culture. When the culture is strong everyone knows what the firm and the team stand for and can act accordingly. In those cases where there is a strong and relevant firm-wide culture then the task of the team is to work out how to 'live' the cultural values in its day-to-day work. In those cases where corporate values are not advocated then it is useful for the team, as part of its strategic thinking, to agree its own appropriate values to guide its behaviour in relation to tasks, colleagues and clients.

A lot of work goes into developing a sound business strategy and creating a strong culture. The first step is to get agreement and commitment within the team.

SHARE TEAM VALUES AND AGREE GROUND RULES

Many organizations these days publish statements of desired values. An example, from law firm DLA, appears in Table 4.1.

They provide a useful backcloth for appropriate behaviour. However, they are only a starting point. To be really effective in pursuing its strategic objectives a team needs to make explicit how these broad values can be translated into standards of behaviour about work and relationships. A vital task for leaders of professional service teams is to encourage a consensus among team members on the responsibilities that they owe to each other, to colleagues outside the team and to the clients. Agreement on the principles governing the operation of a team on a day-to-day basis is also an important part of this process. Once there is agreement then good team leaders remind their people, when necessary, about those values and standards of behaviour. They counsel team members

Table 4.1 The DLA values

People	Service	Quality
We bring the best out of our people by encouraging mutual respect, responsibility and teamwork. We invest in the reputation and careers of all of our people.	We commit to delivering demonstrable value to our clients. We take a broad, business-led view to all client issues. We seek new and innovative solutions to client and market issues.	We strive to achieve the highest quality in everything we do. We meet our professional obligations and take responsibility for our decisions.

who are neglectful. In effective teams, the members as well as the team leader remind colleagues of the standards that are being contravened or only partially observed.

A good starting point is for you to provide time with your people to discuss desirable and undesirable behaviour and formulate agreed ground rules for the future. Because professionals often prefer to work in their own ways, and are frequently reluctant team members, agreed standards of behaviour provide a collective conscience and usually help the team to perform more effectively.

Teams will decide which matters need to be covered by ground rules. They may include:

- obligations to attend meetings;

- punctuality when attending meetings;

- honouring commitments;

- communicating with colleagues when commitments cannot be met for good reasons;

- learning from failures and mistakes rather than allocating blame;

- accepting collective responsibility;

- welcoming and giving new ideas constructive consideration;

- support for others who take risks;

- support for others in tough times;

- respect for the views of others;

- avoidance of interruptions when others are speaking;

- timely response to client queries;

- handling complaints with grace and a lack of defensiveness;

- willingness to cooperate with colleagues;

- providing constructive feedback to colleagues;

- sharing knowledge and skills;

- involving colleagues with clients;

- courtesy to clients including their junior people;

- courtesy to colleagues including junior people;

- being approachable;

- trust;

- willingness to put things right quickly;

- behaving with integrity;

- avoidance of bullying, blaming, political scheming, dumping work, complaining and disrespect;

- avoidance of power or position abuse.

It is very important for discussions to continue until there is a consensus on the issues that need to be covered by behavioural standards. A genuine consensus, where all team members can say 'I might not agree with every precise detail but I can happily live with the general thrust', is much more likely to lead to a commitment from everyone to live by the standards than a majority vote. As a result the standards are more likely to be observed in practice.

It is helpful for standards of behaviour to be defined precisely. For instance, it is more useful to say, 'All team meetings will start at the designated times and participants are expected to arrive five minutes beforehand'. It is less useful to say, 'We should all be punctual as far as attendance at meetings is concerned'. Finally, it is generally helpful for the agreed standards to be available to all team members in writing.

LEAD CHANGE

Professor John Kotter of the Harvard Business School has produced a research-based model for leading major organizational change (1996). Success in his view depends on the implementation of an eight-step process.

The stages, all of which need to be followed sequentially, are as follows:

1. Create a sense of urgency.

2. Put together a team of people to lead the change.

3. Create a vision of the desired outcome and formulate strategies for achieving it.

4. Communicate the desired outcome and strategies.

5. Empower people, throughout, to remove obstacles and implement ideas to improve performance.

6. Identify and reward early benefits.

7. Consolidate gains and produce more change.

8. Weld the new approaches into the firm's culture.

Create a sense of urgency

It is helpful, first, to identify possible causes of complacency. These may include the absence of a visible crisis, the achievement of low performance standards, low candour about problems and favourable performance feedback coming primarily from within.

Raising a sense of urgency is possible by, for instance, eliminating obvious examples of excess; setting goals sufficiently high so that they can't be achieved by business as usual; circulating more data to more people about financial performance and client satisfaction; and tabling more relevant data and having honest discussions at meetings.

Put together a team of people to lead the change

Change, if it is to be effective, needs to be led by a mixture of senior people with strong position power, broad expertise relevant to the task and high credibility. To make change happen they need to create trust through carefully planned off-site events with lots of talk and joint activities.

Create a vision of the desired outcome and formulate strategies for achieving it

An effective vision needs to appeal to both hearts and minds. The end product ideally results in a direction of the future that is desirable, feasible, focused, flexible and communicable.

Communicate the desired outcome and strategies

Communicating the vision and strategies requires repetition and the use of a multimedia approach. The key messages need to be repeated time and again with the use of different vehicles, for example meetings, presentations, speeches, in-house publications and e-mails. It is preferable to use language that is straightforward and jargon free. Inconsistencies should be explained and reactions tested. It is desirable to bring messages alive with stories, examples, metaphors and analogies. Above all, leadership by example is critical. Leaders must behave in a way that is consistent with the vision.

Empower people, throughout, to remove obstacles and implement ideas to improve performance

Get everyone, in their respective teams, to generate ideas to remove barriers to change and to improve performance within the vision and strategy framework. Ideas for improving structures, processes, service and working practices should be encouraged.

Identify and reward early benefits

It is useful to identify, publicize and reward early benefits that accrue during the change process. This encourages everyone to remain enthusiastic about working towards full implementation of the ultimate vision.

Consolidate gains and produce more change

It is helpful to use the credibility afforded by early gains in the change process to tackle additional and bigger projects. It is important to re-emphasize shared purpose and to keep up the spirit of urgency. It is a good idea to involve junior people in more projects to assist the change effort.

Weld the new approaches into the firm's culture

New approaches only become embedded in the culture when it is clear that they work and are superior to old methods. Use lots of talk to hype up the validity of the new practices and promote and reward those who support and implement them.

This model of leading change is, in my view, important to leaders of professional teams in two ways. Although major changes have to be led, as Kotter suggests, by a team of senior people, it is evident that team leaders throughout the firm have a significant part to play in communicating the desired outcomes and strategies. They are also responsible for empowering their colleagues to remove obstacles and implement ideas to improve performance. Furthermore it is desirable for them to have played their part in the formulation of the vision in the first place. It is instructive to see how closely the stages outlined were followed in the successful 'culture change' programme at DMH, described in the case history below, even though the people involved were not aware, at the time, of Kotter's work.

The second reason why the model is helpful is that it may be used as a guide for leading changes that are specifically relevant to the work of your own team. You and your colleagues may wish to make some changes, say, to improve service quality, modify working practices, introduce new team processes or move into new markets. The framework outlined, with minor modifications, should help you to succeed.

CASE HISTORY

Leading change – a new culture at DMH

This case history demonstrates the importance of both a strong lead from the top and effective team leadership throughout the firm.

DMH is a medium-size law firm with offices in Brighton, Crawley, Worthing and London. In 1997 a new managing partner was elected. Together with his colleagues he revolutionized the business. Tim Aspinall, the new Managing Partner, had this to say about the firm before the changes came to fruition:

> The firm had grown over the years into a multi-site operation with seven branches, all but two of which concentrated principally on private client activities. There were very different service values among our lawyers. Some lawyers behaved as individuals who just happened to practise together. There was a tension between the private client activities based around the high street and the commercial activities based around corporate clients. Nobody was prepared to resolve these tensions as it involved difficult decisions being taken. People were very busy generating fees but these were not always translated into profit. Financial rewards were still broadly based on the 'lockstep' principle by which the shares of profits for partners were determined primarily by length of service. We were reasonably successful despite the problems. Local accountants, bankers and other business people said that the firm was underperforming in relation to its potential. The firm was a slumbering giant.

As is often the case, the catalyst for change was a crisis. In 1996 a small group of successful partners who recognized the need for major changes began to contemplate leaving the firm. One of them did leave. Tim Aspinall was encouraged to run for managing partner.

Tim Aspinall described his thoughts:

> I was in two minds. I enjoyed practising law. I was 39 years of age and I had concerns about my future career if I became managing partner at such a young age. On the other hand I had become interested in business, leadership and management. I had some clear ideas about what could be done but I was also worried that the firm might not

be ready for them. In the end, knowing that I had the support of some key people who were, themselves, desperate for change, I decided to accept the challenge. I decided it was an opportunity that might not come again. I told the partners that I would like to do the job and I explained to them how I would like to see the firm change.

Tim Aspinall's manifesto for change was to:

▌ Create a coordinated business with a clear mission and structure.

▌ Significantly develop the more profitable commercial side of the business.

▌ Promote the concept of profitable fee earning rather than the maximization of fee income whether profitable or not.

▌ Close the uneconomic branches.

▌ Set up a matrix of teams composed of legal specialists on the one hand and multidisciplinary teams to serve the needs of particular market sectors on the other.

▌ Reduce, and eventually give up, legal aid work.

▌ Appoint real leaders as heads of departments and teams with accountability and responsibility for results.

▌ Deliver more profit for the partnership.

Tim Aspinall also told his colleagues that in order for the job of managing partner to be valued properly he needed to be rewarded on the basis of his performance as a leader rather than as a lawyer.

In January 1997 the incumbent managing partner, who was nearing the end of his term of service, indicated that he was happy to give way, and Tim Aspinall was invited into office. The partners also voted Derek Sparrow, a corporate law partner, into office as Chairman. Some partners thought that he would act as a check and balance for some of the more radical aims of the new managing partner. Other partners saw him as someone to turn to if they had significant worries about the way things were developing. In the event the chairman was very quickly convinced that the new direction envisaged for the firm was the right one. He gave his full support for all of the developments from January 1997 onwards.

Tim Aspinall knew that the changes that he envisaged would take three years or so to be fully accepted and implemented. He felt strongly that he needed to progress with the consent of the partners, other lawyers and support people and that therefore extensive consultation would be necessary. He realized that he would have to invest a good deal of his own time in the process, to lead by example and to harness the enthusiasm and dedication of professional and support leaders throughout the firm. The first step in 1997 was to appoint a new management board of partners who were sympathetic broadly with the desired changes. This was not too difficult because the firm's constitution allows for managing partners to appoint their own boards. The firm was reorganized into teams of specialist lawyers and multidisciplinary teams to serve market sectors and specific clients. Individuals with evident leadership capabilities or potentiality were selected to lead the teams. Accountabilities were defined for members of the management board and team leaders throughout. An intensive programme of training courses was set up to enhance leadership skills within the context of the desired new culture. Emphasis was placed in these courses on leading change, developing and implementing business team strategies, communications, coaching, motivation, influencing, forging teamwork and dealing with conflicts. Workshops on marketing, selling, financial management and service quality were also held for leaders and team members.

It soon became evident that consultative workshops held every two or three months were making a major contribution to refining the vision and to the establishment of the new culture. Everyone in the firm, professionals and support people, was invited to attend. Participants worked in small groups to evolve the firm's thinking on such matters as service quality, marketing, selling, measuring performance, rewards, conditions for staff and teamwork. In the early days the outcomes of the workshops were largely aspirational. The firm's leaders, with their teams, steadily turned those aspirations into effect, fostered new methods of working and encouraged more appropriate ways of behaving. Ultimately clear cultural values, broadly agreed, evolved to guide the partners and the staff in appropriate ways to tackle jobs, work together and relate to the clients.

New team leaders were appointed to replace those who, although they may have been outstanding lawyers, were less effective in the leadership role. Every effort was made to help those replaced take on other roles within the firm. Tim Aspinall said:

> These days many more young lawyers look forward to becoming team leaders. They know that to become a partner it is now important to be more than a first-class lawyer. They need to be able to develop new business and to lead a team. We think it takes three years or so for qualified lawyers to become really effective professionally. They may then be ready to become a leader of a small team. We no longer feel that it is necessary for a lawyer to be a partner before he or she assumes leadership responsibilities.

DMH has modified its financial reward system so that for both partners and others performance in all aspects of the work is recognized. For team leaders, competence in leading, as well as in legal work, is one of the criteria. Tim Aspinall said, 'This is a very visible way of reinforcing our belief that leadership is critically important'.

DMH has not achieved its changes without a handful of casualties. Tim Aspinall said:

> We had to part company with two or three partners who didn't like the changes and refused to be accountable. It was not easy to do that with partners who earned high fees for the firm. We took the view, however, that if they were opposed, in word and deed, to where the majority of us wanted to go then this outweighed their fee-earning contribution. The buck stopped with me and taking the decision to part company was a risk. The partnership might have voted against. If that had been so it would have been a resigning matter for me. There is a lesson here for identifying and developing leaders in law firms. Lawyers because of their training and professional duties tend to be cautious and risk averse. Leaders have to be the reverse. We have to take this into account in appointing our team leaders at all levels.

DMH has made huge strides since 1997 and now receives many accolades, including being a Legal 500 and Chambers recommended firm. It is a much more profitable business than it was in 1996. It is regarded as an attractive firm in which to work. It has prestigious clients and receives excellent feedback on its service. In Tim Aspinall's view the changes at DMH that are now in place, and working, are because they have team leaders who display the following characteristics:

- They are good professionals, business people and leaders within their own groups and as members of the larger DMH team.

- They accept and promote the principle of collective responsibility whereby once decisions have been made they are enthusiastically supported and put into effect even if they were opposed during the decision-making process.

- They lead by example and 'live' the new cultural beliefs and values.

- They spend a lot of time communicating the new ways of doing things.

- They give a significant amount of time to their leadership responsibilities.

- They are good at coaching people to change and they empower their team members to provide their own ideas for improving performance within the framework of the new developing culture.

- They think that leadership is important and are enthusiastic about the tasks involved

It is clear from DMH's experience that welding major changes into the fabric of a firm requires not only a strong and determined lead from the top but also enthusiastic and competent team leaders at all levels. It is very much a team effort.

5

Communications: Getting the message across, listening and creating the right climate

Give people a fact or idea and you enlighten their minds; tell them a story and you touch their souls.

— (Old Hasidic proverb)

I know that you believe you understand what you think I said, but I am not sure you realize that what you heard is not what I meant.

— (Alan Greenspan)

Getting the message across is more than obtaining understanding. It is also about gaining acceptance. Intelligent professionals and support staff usually want to ask questions and often want to challenge or argue about the message or some aspects of it. Listening therefore is as important in the communication process as the provision of a clear, simple and memorable message. Some leaders mistakenly try to avoid two-way communications. They may fear that their message will be torpedoed. They may resent the time involved. These are understandable reactions but regrettable. Quite simply, if people do not accept the message whether it is about change, performance or behaviour there will be little willingness to turn the communication into action. If feedback indicates that the message is inappropriate or not well thought out then it is preferable for it to be reconsidered. This is better in the long run than persevering with something that people will not willingly implement.

GET THE MESSAGE ACROSS

Here are some guidelines:

▌ *Appeal to hearts and minds.*   Many professionals, especially lawyers, accountants, scientists and engineers, use the power of reason and evidence to persuade others. They use logical arguments, marshal data in support of their proposals and are good at rebutting those points with which they disagree. Articulate leaders can be very effective when communicating in this way. However, there is the risk of failure. An overwhelmingly logical case sometimes intimidates others and may lead to rejection. Appealing to the hearts as well as the minds is often the answer. Messages crafted to 'touch the soul' increase the possibility of acceptance. Stories, examples, illustrations, analogies and metaphors that appeal to the emotions, hopes, values and aspirations of the listeners are an important adjunct to facts and opinions. They help to direct latent energy and enthusiasm into work, problem solving and effecting change. Beware, however, of using old and stale analogies, metaphors and illustrations. Beware especially of resorting to those that have been overused within the firm. They are clichés and may detract significantly from the message.

Ian Pearman, Account Director at advertising agency Abbott Mead Vickers, who peppers his conversations with metaphors, says:

> I believe strongly in the power of analogy. Analogies and metaphors are marvellous for communication. I find that I can get my message across and it is much more likely to stick if I am able to summon up good metaphors. I make a conscious effort to do it. Of course in advertising we are in the communications business but we have to remain vigilant about its importance inside the firm in our day-to-day activities as well. We don't want to fall into the trap of the shoemaker's sons being the worst shod.

Team leaders need to pay as much attention to 'packaging' their messages as to the content. Colourful language, as well as stories and analogies and so on, helps to communicate difficult and new information quickly and effectively. Leaders of teams in advertising agencies and design businesses usually find this quite easy, owing to their professional skills. Those in other sectors often have to work rather harder at creating the 'packaging'. As with all things, practice helps.

▌ _Keep it simple._ Confusion, irritation, suspicion and rejection follow in the wake of communications that are long-winded, clumsy and full of jargon. It is hard work to be clear and concise. It takes more time initially but saves time in the longer run. It is good practice to use everyday words whenever possible even with fellow professionals. Speak and write to express rather than impress. Here are two examples that I have come across recently with suggested alternatives:
  – Instead of saying 'All aspects of the situation should be taken into careful consideration prior to the implementation of corrective action', say instead 'Please don't change anything until you have checked it thoroughly'.
  – Instead of saying 'We are going to facilitate a campaign throughout the firm to improve our service quality through the means of providing engagement letters for our clients which will allow them to perceive how assignments will be handled', say 'In future we are going to send engagement letters to our clients which will tell them what we are going to do and how we are going to do it'.

▌ _Tell it and tell it again and again._ Sir Winston Churchill said: 'If you have an important point to make, don't try to be subtle or clever. Use the pile driver. Hit the point once. Then come back and hit it again. Then hit it a third time; a tremendous whack.'

A few years ago I attended the annual conference of a medium-sized accountancy firm. At the beginning of the meeting the senior partner said a few words. He began to speak about the firm's business plan. One of the partners jumped up, interrupted him and said, 'I didn't know that we had a business plan'. It transpired that the partner had been at the last conference, some 12 months before, and had participated in a discussion about the firm's strategy, objectives and business plan. Extraordinarily, it became clear that in his part of the firm he and his colleagues had got on with their work for 12 months without even referring to the plan. He had forgotten that it existed. When challenged about it later he did recall that after the last conference he had filed all of the documents, which probably included the plan, and had never referred to them again. Clearly there was a failure of leadership in not reminding the partner of the firm's strategy and in failing to encourage him and his colleagues to implement the associated plan in their part of the business.

I have noticed that professionals, being intelligent people dealing with intelligent colleagues, often think that it is necessary only to say something once and it will be implemented. The truth lies elsewhere. Busy people have many demands on their attention and messages usually sink in only after repetition. Good team leaders use a multi-pronged approach for their communications. They convey important messages face to face and one to one with their colleagues. They reinforce their messages at team meetings. They put key points in writing. They link performance reviews, collectively and individually, with intentions that have been previously communicated. They take informal opportunities such as corridor chats, waiting for meetings to start, lunches, a walk to the car park and so on to underscore the important messages that they wish to convey.

▌ *Support your message visually.* Most people are able to understand, accept and retain points more easily if they are supported by simple visual aids. How about having a whiteboard or flip chart in your office so that you can illustrate issues more easily in one-to-one or small-group discussions? When you make a formal presentation to your team you probably use PowerPoint or an overhead projector. If so, there are a few useful things to remember. Keep visuals simple. Avoid too many colours, too many fonts and too much information. ClipArt and shadow formats have been done to death and are boring. Create something fresh. Beware the danger of designing in effects, flourishes and animations for their own sake. Your audience will pay attention to the devices rather than the message. Finally, remember that sometimes building up a picture with old-fashioned flip charts and felt pens supports your message more effectively than the latest trendy software. There is something in the maxim 'The less significant the message the greater the need for a shield of visual gimmickry'.

▌ *Write clearly and concisely.* Although they should never replace oral communications it is sometimes helpful to reinforce important messages in writing. Leaders of professional teams can do no better than keep in mind George Orwell's six elementary rules for journalists (1946):

- Never use a metaphor, simile or other figure of speech that you are used to seeing in print.
- Never use a long word when a short word will do.
- If it is possible to cut out a word, always cut it out.
- Never use the passive where you can use the active.
- Never use a foreign phrase, a scientific word or a jargon word if you can think of an everyday English equivalent.
- Break any of these rules sooner than say something outright barbarous.

Orwell also observed: 'A scrupulous writer in every sentence that he writes will ask himself four questions, thus: what am I trying to say? What words will express it? What image or idiom will make it clearer? Is this image fresh enough to have an effect? And he will probably ask himself two more: Could I put it more shortly? Have I said anything that is avoidably ugly?'

COMMUNICATE BY EXAMPLE

One of the finest ways to communicate desirable behaviour or the need for change is by example. In tough times, when it is necessary to keep an eye on expenses, the senior partner of a very successful architectural practice flies in economy rather than business class. The team leaders in a high-performing accountancy firm have a reputation for always getting to their own and other people's meetings a few minutes before the start. When the managing partner of a top design firm receives letters of complaint from clients she personally replies within one working day. Team leaders in a renowned advertising agency provide 'hands-on' help when their team members' projects are running up against tight deadlines. Furthermore, they put in extra hours alongside their people who are handling the assignments. The leader of a highly regarded in-house scientific research unit invites and receives feedback from his people on how helpful he is to them. For six months each year, the senior partner of a top-flight law firm personally supervises the work of one of the trainees.

The point about all of these examples is that a very clear message is sent to everyone in the firm. The word gets around fast. People everywhere begin to believe that leaders mean what they say. Cynicism, if it exists, begins to disappear. Leadership by example works. It is a concept that is readily understood. Sadly it isn't always put into effect. Too often, much higher-percentage pay increases are provided for those at the top of a firm than for those lower down. Too frequently, the senior partner preaches cost cuts but manages to slip in a personal office refurbishment. Too often, senior people agree ground rules, which include obligatory attendance at meetings, and then find excuses to stay away. If leaders say one thing and do another, is it any surprise that cynicism abounds, morale declines and performance tails off?

LISTEN

Listening well goes to the heart of the professional–client relationship. Most professionals, if asked, say that they are pretty good listeners, as otherwise they would not be able to do their jobs. That is generally true. However, as with most basic skills that we take for granted, there are things that we can do to improve. Since effective communication is a two-way process it is particularly important for team leaders to listen well.

Effective listening involves hearing what is being said, understanding the message and its significance, and communicating that understanding back to the speaker. Good rapport, effective long-term relationships and working well together all depend on good listening. This is such an important part of good leadership that it is useful for us to take stock of our ability. You can test your listening skills quickly and simply by answering the following questions.

When listening to your colleagues do you frequently:

- think about what you want to say next rather than about what the speaker is saying?

- find that your mind wanders to other matters so that you miss what is being said?

- show impatience as you wait for the speaker to finish?

- interrupt?

- spend much more time talking than listening?

- misinterpret what is being said by hearing what you want to hear rather than what is meant?

- offer solutions to the speaker before the problem is fully explained?

- show boredom?

Most of us occasionally behave in these ways. That is forgivable. If you answer yes to any of these questions, because it is a frequent problem, then you may wish to do some work on your listening skills.

The ability to listen well is clearly a valuable attribute in any walk of life. It cements relationships in families, friendships and social circles as well as in business firms. It is crucial for a professional service environment. People like to express their views on what is being done and how and why it is being done. If they don't get a good hearing and if they feel that others, especially those with leadership responsibilities, are not really listening then morale and performance usually suffer.

Some professionals, especially those who have been rigorously trained to think and decide logically, appear rather detached. They don't like to show their emotions. Sometimes they seethe inside about the way things are done or about relationships in the team or in the firm. As a result they may not give of their best. A leader who really listens and is able to unravel deep-seated feelings about problems, slights and worries among team members helps in three ways. First, people get distractions off their chests. Secondly, issues that are aired are easier to resolve. Thirdly, more trust is built between the two people involved.

Here are some tips for listening effectively:

▌ Give full attention and make sure that discussions are not going to be interrupted. Encourage the other person to talk. Show concern and interest and signal to the speaker that you are following the conversation.

▌ Ask helpful questions – get people to elaborate by asking both open and closed questions. Open questions begin with interrogatives, 'who', 'why', 'what', 'when', 'where' and 'how', and are useful for drawing people out. They help to get people to reveal opinions and feelings. They cannot be answered with a simple yes or no. An example is 'What improvements in our client database would help you in your work?' Be careful not to overuse 'why'. It can lead to defensiveness. Closed questions that begin with verbs can be used to obtain more specific answers, for example 'Would more information about the decision makers in our client firms be a valuable addition to our client database?' Questions are also useful for obtaining clarification, for example 'Could you please give me a little more background?' or 'Would you mind explaining that last point in a little more detail?' Questions are important to allow us to learn more but they also demonstrate that we are listening carefully.

▌ Summarize information received by briefly rephrasing. This shows that you are listening and that you understand what is being said. It also allows you to check that you have interpreted the message correctly.

▌ Check understanding by asking the speaker to confirm that you have understood what has been said. Say that you haven't followed the argument, if that is the case, and ask for clarification. It is not an admission of stupidity. It aids comprehension and demonstrates intent listening.

▌ Be aware of your own preconceptions, keep an open mind and try to avoid interpreting messages within your own frame of reference. If, for example, there are aspects of someone's personality that you don't care for, you may inadvertently take less notice of that person's case if you believe that he or she has done something wrong.

FOSTER AN OPEN COMMUNICATIONS CLIMATE

Regular and frank communications between colleagues allow everyone to be better informed about results, proposed changes, day-to-day problems and so on. They also help to develop trust and build better relationships. Here are some suggestions:

▌ Help your team members to recognize and use their colleagues' sources of information. Make sure that you are not the only disseminator of information in meetings. Actively involve others in keeping everyone up to date. Encourage information sharing informally on a day-to-day basis as well as in meetings.

▌ Encourage team members to share and work out problems together.

▌ Let people know in good time about information that affects them. Respond quickly to questions and requests for information. Encourage others to do the same.

▌ Encourage a climate where team members feel comfortable about expressing contrary viewpoints. Open debates on issues, but not personalities, allow for options to be explored thoroughly. Better decisions usually result. People also prefer to work in an environment where their views are considered. Team leaders usually remember to do this with the professionals but, sadly, sometimes forget to do so with the support people.

▌ Make it a significant part of your leadership job to help your team members to gain access to individuals and information that they need from other parts of the firm.

▌ Be generous with information. Give much more than people actually need to do their jobs. Encourage a sense of belonging by avoiding secrets.

▌ Ask your colleagues if they are getting all of the information that they need and want from you. Ask them what else they need to know.

▌ Don't be burdened by the notion of confidentiality other than in very exceptional circumstances. Firms usually suffer much more damage from poor communications than from information getting into the wrong hands.

▌ Pre-empt the grapevine by making sure that your colleagues receive accurate information ahead of garbled versions picked up from others.

▌ If your colleagues like the idea, hold periodic informal no-agenda get-togethers such as team lunches for informal catch-up communications.

▌ Provide monthly activity reports both in writing and at team meetings, to highlight results, potential new clients, progress on new developments, people leaving, people joining, status of projects, achievements of individuals, process changes, reorganizations and so on.

▌ Be frank about things that go wrong. Keep all team members fully in the picture. Encourage them to offer positive ideas on solutions and remedies.

▌ Encourage people to tell you when things are going wrong or when major mistakes have been made. Work with your team members to put things right and help them to learn from mistakes. Let everyone know that the unforgivable sin is to keep quiet. When it happens, take a tough line.

▌ Finally, and probably most important of all, lead by 'walking about'. Talk and listen to people over coffee. Drop by their desks or their rooms and chat for a few minutes. Give some thought beforehand about what has occurred recently and should be passed on. Take the opportunity that informal chats provide to get these small but significant messages across. Find out about how things are going. Take an interest in current work and personal activities. Talk about successes, achievements, hopes and aspirations. Discover what things are troubling people. Yes, this is time consuming but it is the essence of good leadership. You learn, your people learn, problems are nipped in the bud and in the process you build better relationships and establish a higher level of trust.

Team leaders in two very different professional service businesses explain how they foster open communications. David Law, a Pricewaterhouse-Coopers partner leading a team of accountants providing services to the London insurance and investment management sector, says:

> I block out time in the diary on a regular basis to walk the floors. I really do believe that chatting to people, one to one and in small groups, is so very important. It is too easy to hide away in the office. Of course it is a problem to find the time because there is the pressure of client work. You have to be disciplined about it. Getting around the office regularly, for sustained periods, is the only way that I find out what is going on and what is worrying people. It is also a great opportunity for me to get my thinking across to my colleagues. Meetings are fine but I think that this informal contact is better.

Ian Pearman, Account Director at advertising agency Abbott Mead Vickers, puts it this way:

> I think that there are a couple of good things to do to encourage communications in the team. The first is to spend time in touch with everybody, listening and talking. It sounds obvious and it is, but you have to make the effort to get up from your own work and make contact and you have to keep doing it. The second thing is I like to have open debates with the team about assignments, the way we work together, our procedures and so on. I don't mind what people say; in fact, anything goes. I want people to put all sides of the argument. In this way we can keep each other informed. We can work out problems together and we can agree on the best course of action. Sometimes we have these debates in the office and sometimes over lunch. It doesn't matter. The important thing is to set aside time regularly to do it, not in a formal way but just whenever it is necessary.

6

Motivation: Creating the conditions for outstanding performance

When you cease to make a contribution, you begin to die.
— (Eleanor Roosevelt)

Kind words can be short and easy to speak,
but their echoes are truly endless.
— (Mother Teresa)

The drive to behave in a particular way comes from within. Because this is well understood, many leaders of professionals believe that they can have little impact on the motivation of their team members. In fact, good leaders have a major influence on the extent to which their people work with enthusiasm and seek to achieve excellent results. They can play a significant part in improving the motivational climate and in removing obstacles to individual motivation.

There are three useful things that you can do. The starting point is the team leader's own motivation, energy and enthusiasm for achieving results. The example that comes from a strong and focused drive has a positive effect on the motivation of others. Secondly, there are a number of useful leadership skills that, if deployed frequently, can lead to better motivation. Some of these work well with professionals, and others are probably more useful for support people. Some are relevant to both. They are not difficult skills to use. Whether there is the willingness to use them is another matter. Thirdly, it is evident that most of us have preferences for working in particular ways and for tackling some tasks rather than others. Allowing for flexibility in working methods, as long as service quality and output are not hindered, helps to maintain a high level of motivation. Matching assignments to passions fosters a good motivational climate.

DEMONSTRATE YOUR OWN DRIVE FOR RESULTS

Energetic and enthusiastic leaders who demonstrate a vigorous drive for results have a positive effect on their team members. They act as role models. There are a number of things that you can do:

- Make sure that your team members, individually and collectively, have a clear sense of direction and challenging objectives for the more important things that need to be done.

- Monitor team and individual results frequently. Give praise and thanks for goals achieved. Help your people to learn from failures and take remedial action.

- Give time and attention to making sure that there are first-class processes in place to support the drive for outstanding results.

- Celebrate accomplishments with team members and challenge them to do even better.

- Convey a sense of enthusiasm about your team's work to people both inside and outside your team.

- Set aside some time to help with assignments that are running into unanticipated difficulties. This means really helping with a 'hands-on' contribution, not just warm words and encouragement.

- Encourage team members to help each other to overcome obstacles. Bring people together to generate ideas and solve problems when individual team members are running into major problems on their assignments.

▌ Keep the attention of team members focused on the priority activities that provide the best returns.

▌ Finally, and perhaps most important of all, display energy and enthusiasm, all of the time, in your own professional and leadership work. Yes, even when it is the last thing that you feel like doing!

GIVE RECOGNITION FOR PERFORMANCE

It is sad but true that many people, senior as well as junior, go through their working lives without receiving any kind of personal appreciation or recognition. Whenever I speak with leaders of teams of professionals it is clear that they are perfectly well aware of the importance of positive feedback but in many cases somehow fail to get round to providing it to their people. Sometimes they seem to be too preoccupied with other things. Some people feel embarrassed about expressing appreciation. Others worry that it is seen as false or insincere.

There are some people, apparently very self-assured, who make it clear that they do not need positive feedback from colleagues. They may find that the feedback that they get from clients is sufficient for their needs. In other cases they claim to know when they have done a good job and that is sufficient satisfaction. However, I suspect that these people are very much the exceptions to the general rule.

Here are some tips for giving recognition:

▌ Don't 'debase the coinage' by giving recognition as a matter of routine or when it is not deserved.

▌ Give recognition for high-quality service to clients; for meeting very tight deadlines; for initiatives taken; for helping colleagues; for accomplishing more than is promised; for learning new skills; for contributions that go beyond normal work activities; and for exceeding targets.

▌ Give authentic praise that is specific rather than general and is supported with the reasons why you are pleased.

▌ Give thanks for particular contributions with reasons.

▌ Let senior colleagues know about exceptional accomplishments by individuals or groups within your team.

▌ If your firm has a house magazine arrange for deserving team members and their achievements to be featured.

▌ Celebrate major team successes, for instance by going out for dinner together.

▌ Circulate regular reports of team achievements including feedback from clients; successful financial performance; individual accomplishments; new clients engaged; lessons learnt; and major new initiatives.

▌ Be sensitive to the type of recognition with which each of your team members is comfortable and behave accordingly. For example, some people respond well to receiving praise or thanks in front of colleagues whilst others much prefer a quiet word.

Finally, remember to give recognition and appreciation to the support people in the team for their particular accomplishments as well as to the professionals. And include them in the celebrations of team successes.

INCREASE RESPONSIBILITY

In professional service teams the more senior people, for instance partners and associates, usually have all of the responsibility and authority that they need to undertake their work. On the other hand the more junior professional employees and the support people may feel over-controlled and consequently dissatisfied. Often, in these circumstances, people respond very well to being able to take decisions on matters previously requiring the approval of the team leader. Of course you may have to help them to develop some new skills to cope with the extra responsibility.

PROVIDE MORE INTERESTING
AND CHALLENGING WORK

A failure to delegate properly is not uncommon, especially, but not exclusively, in law firms. In other words a large proportion of the professional work time of more senior people is spent doing things that more junior team members, with the right coaching, supervision and support, could handle. This not only means lower profits as a result of having a high-cost delivery system but it also slows down the development of skills and reduces morale and motivation among the juniors. The lack of interesting and challenging work usually results in higher staff turnover than otherwise.

Chris Lucas, a PricewaterhouseCoopers partner leading a team of accountants providing services to the banking and capital markets sector, is clear about this:

> In my view people should be doing work with which they are only just comfortable. Giving challenging work to people as early as possible in their careers is a great way to move them up the learning curve. It is an excellent investment for the firm and good for the morale of the individual. But you have to be available to provide support. It is a bit like a parent encouraging a child to swim by walking backwards in the water with arms outstretched ready to catch hold of the child should the need arise.

Here are some ideas for ensuring that junior professionals get more interesting and challenging work:

▌ If you have the authority, encourage your senior team members to agree lower targets for personal chargeable or billable hours and more hours for supervision, coaching and personal development. By giving more time to coaching and supervision, the senior people will be able to delegate with greater confidence. By giving more time to their personal development they will be able to improve their own professional skills to concentrate on higher-value client activities. Juniors and seniors benefit.

▌ Keep an eye on how your senior colleagues schedule the more junior people for assignments. Encourage them to keep in mind the need for skill development as well as for matching existing abilities to the demands of the tasks and the needs of the clients.

▌ Help your junior professionals to understand the purpose and meaning of tasks. On most assignments there are a number of exciting analytical, creative and communicating activities. There are also plenty of rather mundane progress-chasing, record-keeping, calculating and form-filling tasks. Help your junior professionals to put the less exciting work into context, to understand its importance and to realize that it is worthy of

professional effort. It is possible to have pride in doing relatively routine tasks well when the significance is understood. It is often these
tasks, when poorly executed, that lead to a reputation for poor service
and the possible loss of clients.

EMPHASIZE THE INTERDEPENDENCE OF EVERYONE'S WORK

In professional teams responsibilities vary in terms of range and complexity. However, everyone is part of the team. Everyone's work is
important. It is a sad fact that in professional environments this is
not always recognized. Sometimes a 'them and us' attitude between
professionals and support people is evident. Sometimes professionals
do not acknowledge sufficiently the contributions that the support
people make.

Here are some thoughts on how to demonstrate that everyone's work
is important:

▌ Let everyone know how their contributions impact directly on the
quality of service to clients and how their responsibilities fit into the
team's effort.

▌ Introduce support people to clients when they make visits to the
office.

▌ Involve all team members in meetings, at which, for instance, assignments or projects are being planned. This way they can see how their
work fits in.

▌ When celebrating successes, emphasize the work of the support people.
For example, highlight how the quality of word-processed documents
and their delivery on time contributed to a first-class outcome.

▌ Seek the ideas of all colleagues for improving team working practices
and administrative processes.

▌ As team leader, if you are aware that one or two of your professional
colleagues behave in a rather abrupt, perfunctory or superior manner
towards support people then don't let it go! Take them on one side and
give them some feedback. But do it sensitively (see Chapter 7).

When all team members know that their work is valued and recognized as making a major contribution to success then you have the foundation stone in place for good performance.

ENCOURAGE THE PROVISION OF IDEAS

Most professionals and support people welcome the opportunity to provide ideas for doing new things and for doing things better. These may be concerned with services, processes, systems or structures. They may be relevant to client service, marketing, organization, information technology, management, relationships or the firm's culture. Tapping the ideas that people have about improving performance has two pay-offs. Good ideas that are implemented clearly benefit the firm. Giving people the opportunity to put forward their ideas creates a sense of belonging and being valued beyond the contributions of the day-to-day job. Senior professionals expect to be able to contribute their thoughts on these matters. Good team leaders tap their thinking but also seek out the ideas of junior professionals and support people.

There are some important points to bear in mind. The starting point is to make it known you are always keen to receive ideas on improving the team's or the firm's performance. However, that is not enough. It is beneficial also to provide time for team members to work together to generate and evaluate ideas. As well as being motivational, brainstorming and similar sessions, when well handled, enhance teamwork. They invariably give rise to one or two valuable ideas that can be implemented. More thoughts on how to use teams to generate and evaluate ideas are given in Chapter 8.

Beware, however, of the demoralizing effects of encouraging the provision of ideas but failing to implement the good ones. Beware also of failing to explain why those ideas that can't be implemented for whatever reason are not being progressed.

GET TO KNOW YOUR TEAM MEMBERS
REALLY WELL

I have noticed that many leaders of professional service teams do a lot of the formal things that are required of them. They hold meetings to review performance, they conduct performance review interviews, they keep their people informed about major changes, they involve their teams in objective setting and so on. What they don't do so much of is listening and talking informally one to one with their colleagues.

The motivational effects of taking an interest in people's personal lives, knowing about their aspirations and helping them with their worries and crises cannot be overestimated. It is all about developing relationships that go beyond the day-to-day tasks that people have to do.

I sometimes hear professionals, particularly older ones, say that they haven't the time or the inclination to talk to people other than on strictly technical and business matters. Sometimes they even seem to be a little uncomfortable when out of the strictly professional role. On the other hand leaders who do show a genuine interest in the leisure interests and home and family life of others find that it helps people to feel valued. When this happens then motivation is usually enhanced.

Most young professionals are not simply concerned with their current range of work activities. They have aspirations. If they are in private practice they may want to become partners. Some will want to take on leadership roles. Others will be keen to develop their marketing skills. Many will wish to widen the horizons of their professional abilities by working in new client sectors, pursuing an international presence or developing a different technical speciality. In many firms these issues receive some attention, often mechanical and perfunctory, at annual performance review discussions. Good leaders, however, talk about them frequently and informally with the people concerned. They not only know about their team members' aspirations but they go out of their way to assist in their achievement. People like working for team leaders who are genuinely interested in their career development. It is another key to good motivation. Leaders who have a reputation for helping their people to build their careers are more likely to attract good people to work for them. This is a refreshing contrast to those nominal team leaders who block progress of their good people because they are afraid of losing them to other parts of the business.

We all have our ups and downs in life. We have crises in our personal lives. We become stressed. We get tired. We get frustrated. We have periods when our work doesn't run smoothly. We have tough times with difficult clients. Sometimes these problems lead to a fall-off in performance. Sometimes people try to make up for the difficulties by working extremely long hours. Good leaders are attentive to these crises. By keeping in touch and taking the time, informally, to talk with their colleagues they know when these problems arise. If you are a team leader who is aware, who listens, who offers support and who helps then that will lift the spirits of those experiencing difficulties in their lives and assist them in getting back on track.

Ed Smith explains the importance of this leadership attribute at PricewaterhouseCoopers:

> These days we work in difficult markets. Clients are very demanding. Life is getting more and more complicated. We all need plenty of resilience to cope with the tough conditions. The support that team leaders can provide to their colleagues is vital in ensuring a high level of motivation. We tell our people not to go it alone. There is no sin in asking for help, quite the reverse. What is not acceptable is for people not to ask for help and then to get it wrong. Our team leaders know that they must always be available to provide support. In a way, availability to colleagues, when help is needed, is the essence of the team leader's role. I believe that it is a key factor in how we keep people motivated.

CREATE AN ENJOYABLE WORK ENVIRONMENT

Most professionals enjoy their technical work and get a kick out of serving their clients well. However, when I visit some offices where groups of professionals are at work, I notice that the atmosphere is rather leaden. Conversations, few and far between, are serious. There is very little smiling. There are lots of heads down behind closed doors. Telephone chats lack animation. People wander through the corridors with glum faces. It is as though they all believe that you can't have hard work and fun at the same time. I am sure that these groups get their work done. But I wonder if a creative sparkle is missing. I wonder whether conversations with clients and colleagues are just at the level of getting by. Fortunately the scene that I have painted here is the exception rather than the rule and, to be fair, I have never come across it in advertising and design firms.

It is clear to me that it is possible for people to combine hard work with fun and when they do that they are usually more creative and enthused to perform well. In short, they tend to be well motivated. Leadership by example is critical here. If you can laugh at yourself, exchange a joke or two, engage in some small talk, tell the odd amusing story about your professional work, listen to the light-hearted banter of colleagues and generally lighten the atmosphere you will almost certainly encourage others to do the same. There will be an increase in motivation all round. If you want your people to be creative and go the extra mile for service quality then making the effort to develop and maintain an enjoyable working environment for your team is a must. Fortunately all of this comes naturally to most people but some have to work at it. A word of warning is appropriate. Making team members the butts of one's humour is often demoralizing to the people concerned. 'Pulling legs' is probably best done with people you know really well and with whom you have a very good relationship. This is especially true if you are the team leader.

INSPIRE PEOPLE TO PROVIDE OUTSTANDING SERVICE

Good leaders can inspire team members to excel by fostering optimism and a positive outlook. Here are some practical tips:

▌ Create a virtuous circle of positive expectations. Expect your team members to perform well. People are then more likely to live up to them.

▌ Lead by example. Make sure that your own professional work and client relations are models of excellence.

▌ Show particular appreciation and give recognition to efforts that go beyond the call of duty. Do the same for those who surmount difficult obstacles and who achieve outstanding results.

▌ Use positive and optimistic language. Convey the belief that problems can be overcome and work with your people to find solutions.

▌ Nurture people's creative abilities by building on their ideas and encouraging them to build on yours.

▌ Encourage people to be impatient with the status quo and to look continually for better ways of doing things.

When we talk of inspirational leaders we usually think of statesmen like Winston Churchill or John Kennedy or leaders of subjugated people like Martin Luther King and Nelson Mandela. They all told powerful stories. They all had the gift of language and a way with words that truly gripped people's attention and encouraged action. Leaders of professional service teams usually inspire in a less dramatic way. The useful attributes are probably energy, enthusiasm and taking a genuine interest in others. Listening well, good humour and the ability and willingness to nurture people's creative spirits are important accompaniments.

PLAY TO PEOPLE'S PASSIONS

Most professionals enjoy their technical work. After all, they chose the career in the first place primarily because they were attracted to the work involved and felt that it suited their abilities and personalities. Of course most people get bored if they do the same work for too long. That is why it is so necessary for professionals to widen and deepen their skills as their careers progress. We have already seen how important it is for team leaders to provide help and encouragement.

In most professional teams there are many tasks, beyond the technical work, that have to be undertaken. It is here that good leaders tap the enthusiasm of their people by playing to their passions. For example, some people love the opportunity to appear in front of others and make presentations. Others hate it. Some people enjoy getting their teeth into a project that will lead to better ways of doing things. Others find it a distraction. Some people get a huge kick out of helping others with their work and their careers. Others get impatient. If people love doing the work then they generally do it well. If they need to improve their skills then they usually make it their business to do so. Good leaders know the activities that 'turn their people on' and match assignments accordingly.

Here are some examples of activities best undertaken by those who have a passion for doing the work involved. It is an opportunity to play to people's strengths:

▌ making formal presentations to potential clients to win business;

▌ networking and building relationships to promote business opportunities;

▌ writing articles that help to develop the reputation of the individual, the team and the firm;

▌ contributing to seminars that help to build the reputation of the individual, the team and the firm;

▌ leading or contributing to internal projects – examples might include developing and implementing new systems, producing proposals for exploiting new markets and designing questionnaires for obtaining formal feedback on service quality from clients;

▌ mentoring and supervising trainees;

▌ running internal training sessions;

▌ facilitating sessions for generating and evaluating ideas;

▌ organizing promotional events;

▌ doing some research on an industry, geographical market or potential client;

▌ helping with the recruitment and selection process;

▌ chairing meetings.

KEEP IN MIND THE DISTINCTION BETWEEN EXTRINSIC AND INTRINSIC INCENTIVES

Various pieces of research, including those by Frederick Herzberg (2003) and Harry Levinson (2003), have shown clearly the importance of distinguishing between extrinsic incentives like pay and conditions and the intrinsic ones that lie deep within human nature. Ask people what makes them dissatisfied at work and you hear about poor pay, irritating bosses, uncomfortable working environments, unfairness and inappropriate rules, red tape and bureaucracy. Managed badly, these factors make people fed up and are likely to be demoralizing. But when managed well, they do not necessarily motivate individuals to excel. People are more likely to be motivated to perform well if they have interesting work, more responsibility rather than less, challenging assignments, an opportunity to develop their skills and recognition for their efforts. These intrinsic factors answer people's deep-seated needs for growth and achievement.

It is clearly desirable for firms to provide competitive pay and benefits. It is also sensible to provide good personnel policies and procedures, a decent working environment and to avoid stupid rules, red tape and bureaucracy. These help to prevent dissatisfaction, poor performance and high staff turnover. However, when they are in place they do not, by themselves, guarantee a high level of motivation and a desire to excel. They are necessary but not sufficient. For outstanding performance to occur, team leaders have a crucial role to play. It is their job to ensure that team members are engaged in interesting and challenging work assignments. They can help people to develop their skills. They can look for ways of providing team members with more responsibility. They can provide opportunities for everyone in the team to generate ideas. They can make sure that people receive recognition for good performance. In other words it is the job of the firm's top management to ensure that the extrinsic incentives like competitive pay and decent personnel policies are in place. On the other hand it is very much the task of team leaders throughout the firm to search, continually, for ways of improving those intrinsic incentives that can reach deeply into people's psychological make-up and bring the best out of them.

Managing Partner Tim Solomon has this to say about the intrinsic motivators at advertising agency Ogilvy & Mather:

> In advertising a prime motivator is the work itself. It is fun and it is exciting. Feedback comes to everybody, formally and informally, from the clients and through the figures. So, everyone knows how she or he is doing. Good team leaders are well aware of the motivational effect of the work. They can give people a bit more room to deliver. They can keep raising the bar. They can encourage people to stretch themselves.
>
> Team leaders who are enthusiastic and energetic radiate excitement. I believe that this helps motivation. Undoubtedly the opposite is true. Glum leaders very quickly spread gloom and despondency among their colleagues. Even when life is tough an attitude of things will get better helps. Walking the halls, sitting on people's desks for an informal chat, being truthful, not over-promising and building trust are all important for motivation.
>
> If individuals lose some of their motivation then our team leaders provide help. It might be a matter of assisting with skill development through coaching. Our world is a high-pressure one. If people feel a bit low because things have not been going too well it is the team leader's job to provide support and to get team colleagues to help to lift them. So in one way and another although the nature of the work is the key to motivation there are many things that team leaders can do to help things along.

Development Director Alison Chadwick and Account Director Ian Pearman at advertising agency Abbott Mead Vickers also provide insights about intrinsic motivators. This is what Alison Chadwick has to say:

> The opportunity for advancement is central to motivation here, in terms of promotion, but also through the work that people are involved in. We believe that giving people more responsibility and fresh challenges is a strong motivator. We take long-term career development very seriously, and we are always looking for ways of stretching people. As part of this, team leaders are

expected to listen to people's ideas. We also place great emphasis on recognizing good performance. It is a day-to-day responsibility of individual team leaders to acknowledge good performance, but praise for teams and individuals also comes through memos from senior management that are circulated throughout the agency. This recognition is often for achievements such as new business pitches won. However, if for example a pitch is lost but the efforts to win it have been good, this is still publicly recognized. We believe recognizing talent and effort is a critical factor in sustaining motivation and morale. Other ways of appreciating people's contributions are also encouraged. For example, team leaders sometimes give flowers or other gifts for good work or significant effort. Some departments also give regular awards to highlight excellent performers. Overall we try to provide a challenging environment for everyone to achieve their potential, and plenty of support to encourage them along the way.

Ian Pearman adds further thoughts:

When we are going through a tough time it is part of the leadership job to create momentum. It is too easy to fall into the trap of gloom and despondency. Instead we have to create a virtuous circle by focusing on things that are going right and stressing that things will get better. This lifts people and we stand a much better chance of making some good progress as a result. Our approach to motivation is to emancipate people from fear. We believe in very much more carrot than stick. We all make mistakes. We try to learn from them and give support rather than castigate. As a result people feel sorry and a bit guilty when they make mistakes. They feel that they have let the side down and are keen to make amends. Of course we work out between us how to avoid similar mistakes in the future. This sort of reassurance and support is good for motivation. There is, however, one thing that we are tough on. That is arrogance and spikiness. It is an important part of our value system that people treat each other decently. We are usually successful at picking up the important qualities of courtesy, humility, openness and willingness to listen at the selection stage. Occasionally people slip through, behave wrongly, and then we make it very clear that it is unacceptable.

7

Coaching: Helping team members to get the best out of themselves

---

I like to think that the same holds true for tennis strokes: that the perfect strokes are already within us waiting to be discovered, and that the role of the pro is to give a nudging encouragement. One reason I like to think this is that when my students think of strokes as being discovered rather than manufactured, they seem to learn the game much faster and without frustration.

— (W Timothy Gallwey)

Learning is not compulsory. Nor is survival.

— (W Edwards Deming)

I am sometimes told that professionals do not need to be coached. They are intelligent, well-educated and motivated individuals who can be relied upon to be outstanding performers. I suspect that this sentiment is wrong for a number of reasons. In the majority of cases professionals are indeed knowledgeable, skilful and enthusiastic about their work. Like talented sports players, however, they are more likely to build on their strengths, fulfil their potentiality and accomplish outstanding results if an effective coach supports them. The second reason is that performance is sometimes not up to scratch. An individual may lack a critical skill, have an undesirable approach to work or colleagues, lack confidence or be unwilling, for the time being, to put enough effort into the job. An effective coach can play a useful part in helping to overcome these difficulties. The third reason why coaching is important is that we live in a fast-changing world. Professionals are just as exposed as everyone else to new competitive threats, developments in information technology, changes in client attitudes and behaviour and new economic and political influences. Good coaches help to give people the confidence to cope with our ever-changing business and professional environment. Lastly, coaching can play a useful part in helping younger people to think through their longer-term career aspirations. Most of us find it beneficial to use an experienced and respected colleague as a sounding board. The coach, who in this context is sometimes described as a mentor, may also help with introductions to other people who in their turn provide assistance, in one way or another, with career development.

YOU HAVE TO WANT TO HELP

Coaching is about *helping* other people to learn and to put their learning into effect. Notice the emphasis on the word 'helping'. Managerial leaders do not always see their work in this light. One said to me 'I leave that sort of thing to trainers, teachers and counsellors. I have a job to get on with.' Professionals and their support colleagues are knowledge workers. They are expensive assets. The willingness to invest personally in the development of people goes to the heart of the leadership role. However, it is not only about investment. There must also be a genuine desire to help others to fulfil themselves for its own sake if it is going to be done well.

Most people who are good at coaching say that they enjoy the experience. They take pleasure in seeing others make progress. They also find it a rewarding learning experience for themselves. They learn more about other people and their jobs. They enhance their own skills in the process and they often learn more about themselves generally.

Perhaps you don't coach at the moment but you are thinking of starting. If so, here is a cautionary word or two. To be effective you really do have to believe in the value of helping others. You really do have to want to do it. You are unlikely to be successful if you simply learn the skills of coaching and apply them in a mechanical fashion. Integrity is crucial. I go as far as to say that if helping colleagues does not give you a 'buzz' then it would be better to leave the leadership role to others and concentrate on your professional work instead.

Paul Sharp, Head of Organization Development at Pricewaterhouse-Coopers, provides these insights:

> We have learnt that what people value most in those who coach them is a genuine desire to help. They ask themselves three questions. Is the coach really interested in me and in the issue that we are discussing? Is the coach really listening to what I have to say? Is the coach influenced by what I am saying? The respect for and commitment to the individual being coached is fundamental.
>
> Capable professionals by definition are good with clients. If you are good with clients then you probably have the ability to coach. In many cases we just have to help leaders to recognize that the skills are there and simply need to be used in a different context. In the end much of it comes down to the willingness to use good relationship skills for the benefit of team members and their performance just as much as to use them with clients.
>
> Professionals tend to have very high expectations of themselves. Accountants especially have had lots of training in spotting the imperfections. They often turn the spotlight on to themselves. They amplify the weaknesses. They magnify the Achilles heel. In some ways this can mean that the most talented professionals create the most insecurities for themselves. Therefore often the role of the coach is to invite the subjects to place the spotlight on their strengths as a basis for building confidence.

BUILD THE RIGHT RELATIONSHIP

Mutual respect and trust are at the core of a good relationship between a coach and a learner in any field of endeavour. Team leaders in professional service firms earn their respect by doing their leadership job well. That includes coaching. Their competence and achievements as professionals also play a part. It is probably true to say that they do not have to be among the best performers technically. As in sport and music, for instance, the learner is often more proficient professionally than the coach. Respect for the coach also depends on the way that the job is carried out. If learners believe that the coach is there genuinely to help rather than to show off, criticize or embarrass then respect follows. We all remember schoolteachers whom we respected and those whom we did not. Those who inspired and helped us are usually recalled with affection. We remember and despise those who were sarcastic, abusive and, in my day, gratuitously violent for just those failings. Respect for the coach is a function of the coach's respect for the learner.

Mutual trust results in part from mutual respect. If the person being coached is unable to ask for help when needed; is uncomfortable or defensive with feedback; is unable to talk frankly about aspirations, achievements, mistakes and worries; and finds it difficult to relate on an even footing then there is insufficient trust. It takes time and effort to build trust. It is a part of the broader leadership role. It means taking a genuine interest in others and caring about them; being honest; showing appreciation; revealing your own values, aspirations, interests, concerns and mistakes; and working through problems together before they have time to fester.

RAISE AWARENESS AND GENERATE RESPONSIBILITY

Those who coach for a living develop a wide repertoire of useful skills. As a busy leader of a professional service team you are probably looking for a few basic ideas to help you to enlarge your natural talents to help others to learn. Asking effective questions is the starting point. John Whitmore in his very readable book, *Coaching for Performance* (1993), provides an excellent understanding of the prime importance of asking good questions and offers a simple and memorable framework for putting them into effect. He demonstrates how an approach that works in sport is also appropriate in the world of business and in the public and voluntary sectors. Helping people to learn by asking questions is not new. After all Socrates, some 2,000 years ago, taught by asking questions. Whilst telling is not wrong, there is ample evidence that it is overused. Asking effective questions to help people to learn is correspondingly underused.

Whitmore shows that in sport the purpose of asking questions when coaching is twofold. It is first to raise awareness, and especially self-awareness, of body sensations during a sporting activity. When, by asking questions, attention is drawn to discomforts and inefficiencies in movement they can be reduced and perhaps eliminated. The result is a more fluid and efficient tennis stroke, golf swing or ski turn that takes account of the performer's body size and shape. The second and connected reason for the sport coach to ask questions is to generate responsibility on the part of the performer to decide what to do and then to do it. This is based on the simple fact that motivation cannot be imposed from without but rather comes from within. If performance is to improve then the sportsperson has to take responsibility for bringing it about. The same reasoning applies to performance in the firm. The coach can use questions to help to raise awareness of the current and desired levels of knowledge, skills and behaviour. Questions can also be asked to generate responsibility on the part of the person being coached to decide what action, from possible options, needs to be taken and for putting that action into effect.

The idea is that self-analysis, with help given by the questions from the coach, leads quickly to self-awareness and the acceptance of responsibility for personal development. This is achieved more easily than if the learner is told what to do and how to do it. John Whitmore illustrates this with an example from coaching tennis (1993):

> Watch the ball is the number one instruction in tennis, but it invariably irritates the player and only produces an improvement for a ball or two. 'Watch the ball, I said. How many times do I have to tell you to watch the ball?' It is all so predictable. But if the coach were to ask you which way is the ball spinning as it crosses the net, how high over the net is it this time, can you see the point of contact between the ball and the racket, or how many times do you see the maker's name on the ball after it bounces, what would you do? Yes, in order to answer the question, you would have to look at the ball and you would go on looking at the ball so long as new questions were coming. You are even likely to become so fascinated with the new awareness you have found that you will continue to focus upon the ball to a high quality long after the questions have ceased. It is the question that focuses the attention and increases the awareness, not the much more limited command to 'watch the ball'.

Similarly good questions focus attention in a business context. How many outstanding billings are there? What were the best features of the last assignment? What is the biggest problem that you are thinking about currently? In what ways will you be affected by the new European legislation? Questions to help to generate responsibility might include the following. When will you be able to complete this by? Which of these three options will you go for? What obstacles are there to achieving the target date? How long will it take you to get up to speed? Most people will tackle tasks with more enthusiasm and pay more attention to quality if there is a sense of ownership. Conversely if they are told what to do and it doesn't work there may be excuses. The coach will have failed to generate responsibility.

Whitmore suggests (1993) that the most effective coaching questions for raising awareness and generating responsibility are those that begin with the interrogatives, 'what', 'where', 'when', 'who', 'how much' and 'how many'. He discourages the use of 'why' since it often implies criticism and causes defensiveness. He recommends expressing 'why' questions in the form of 'what were the reasons . . . ?' He recommends that questions should be broadly based to begin with and then should steadily focus on details. The process is rather like peeling the layers off an onion until the centre is revealed.

Generally questions should follow the interests and train of thought of the person being coached. This helps to foster responsibility on the part of the learner. If an important area or aspect is being avoided then the coach may bring it to the foreground by a question along the lines of 'I notice that you have not mentioned . . . Is there any particular reason for this?'

A useful framework, based on Whitmore's work (1993), appears in the box 'The GROW framework'. It is rooted in the mnemonic 'GROW', which stands for 'goal, reality, options and will'. Its value rests on its simplicity. You will use it to best effect, however, if you keep the two reasons for asking questions in the forefront of your mind. Remember they are to raise the learner's awareness about the current situation and future possibilities and to generate responsibility for decisions and actions. Without this context there is a very real danger that following the GROW model will be a mechanical exercise and will produce less than satisfactory results.

Clearly, asking questions is not much use if we don't listen to the replies. Sadly, it needs saying because some of us don't really listen after asking a question; we just wait to ask the next one. The section on listening in Chapter 5 is just as relevant to the process of coaching as to the other aspects of communication.

THE GROW FRAMEWORK

The GROW framework provides a guide to the sorts of questions that the coach can ask the learner. The purpose is to raise the learner's awareness of personal development needs and to encourage responsibility for setting learning goals and formulating realistic action plans to turn them into action. The definitions are:

▌ **G Goal**

Setting goals for the learning assignment in general and/or for this particular coaching session.

▌ **R Reality**

Raising awareness of the current situation.

▮ O Options

Identifying different ways of resolving the problem or achieving the learning goals.

▮ W Will

What is to be done and the will to do it.

Examples of questions for use with the framework:

▮ *Goal*
- What exactly do you want to achieve?
- By when do you want to achieve it?
- How much of this is within your control?
- Is the goal measurable, attainable and challenging?
- Do you want to set milestones against which to measure progress towards your goal?
- What do you suggest?

▮ *Reality*
- What is the situation now?
- What changes would you like to experience?
- What effect does the current situation have on your emotions, morale, motivation, energy and enthusiasm?
- How would you rate yourself, now, in relation to your goal, for example on a 1–10 scale?
- What have you done so far to move towards your goal?
- What is stopping you from moving on from the present position?
- What have you learnt from that?

▮ *Options*
- What are the different things that you could do to reach your goal?
- What else? What else? What else?
- If time were not a factor what could you do?
- If resources were not a factor what could you do?
- What would happen if you did nothing?
- Is there anybody whom you admire who does this well? What does this person do that you could try?

- Would you like another suggestion?
- What are the pros and cons of the options that you have identified?

▌ *Will*
- Which of the options will you choose?
- How does this help you to achieve your goal?
- When are you going to do it?
- How will you know when you have reached your goal?
- What obstacles could you face?
- How will you overcome them?
- What help and support do you need from me or from others?
- When will you take your first step?
- What is the likelihood of you taking this action? (Rate yourself on a 1–10 scale.)

You do not need to follow the above sequence. You may prefer to start with 'Reality' and move on to 'Goal'. The questions listed here are for illustration only. It is best to choose your own.

There are a number of possible outcomes for the learner from a successful coaching session based on the GROW framework. These are:

▌ The learner gains a completely fresh way of looking at a problem or a longer-term learning assignment and takes the appropriate action.

▌ One or two insights or new angles emerge that can be incorporated into future behaviour.

▌ An existing well-thought-out course of action is confirmed and, as a result, there is an increase in confidence to proceed.

All of the outcomes are useful. In each case the coaching session based on the GROW framework is the starting point. The good coach usually stays in touch. It may be appropriate to give some specific guidance during the implementation phase or to arrange for it to be given elsewhere. It may be necessary to approve release and funding for a training course and to review the learning that has occurred and the proposed action to be taken. It may be desirable to lend a hand in planning further learning events such as a research project or shadowing a skilled performer engaged in,

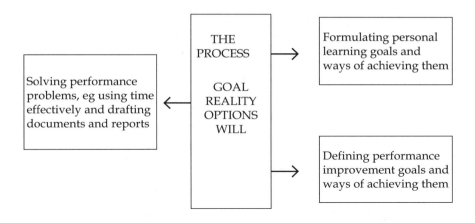

Figure 7.1   Applications of the GROW framework

say, a negotiation, sales pitch or assignment debriefing. The continuing process of learning and action will certainly require periodic discussions involving two-way feedback. These issues are covered in more detail in later sections of this chapter. Meanwhile Figure 7.1 provides a summary of the applications of the GROW framework.

Here are some final words on questions, listening and helping. At PricewaterhouseCoopers, coaching is a serious business. UK Board Member Ed Smith says:

> We invest in the development of coaching skills for our team leaders. Two important abilities are to be able to ask really good questions that go to the heart of the matter and to listen. Accountants are trained to be analytical and critical. Too much of that is dangerous in the leadership context so we make a big effort to accentuate the positives. We use a number of tools to help such as the Myers Briggs personality inventory to help team leaders to learn more about themselves and other people. Coaching is a matter of helping people to be more effective in their careers. We believe that the insights gained from Myers Briggs result in coaching sessions that are conducted with greater sensitivity.

Coaching is also an important part of leadership at Abbott Mead Vickers. Development Director Alison Chadwick has this to say:

> We find coaching an effective and motivating way of helping people to learn in order to improve their performance. We are working with our team leaders to help them develop their

coaching skills. The emphasis, in practice, is on effective questioning, listening and feedback, taking the time to help those being coached build their awareness and take responsibility for the changes they will make. In a way it is a joint problem-solving approach. When coaching, the leader doesn't provide the answers but helps people find their own way forward.

TAKE ACCOUNT OF
DIFFERENT WAYS OF LEARNING

When you are in your coaching role you may find yourself helping a team member to decide on the best way to learn a new skill. This is likely to be in response to a need that has been identified in an earlier or current coaching session. Research by Honey and Mumford (1992) shows that we each have preferred ways of learning. Their work is based, in turn, on Kolb's interactive learning cycle (1984). A derivation is shown in Figure 7.2.

We have an experience that may be intended or may simply happen. If we learn from that experience, consciously or not, we reflect and perhaps gather further information. We then draw conclusions. In the process we formulate frameworks, models or theories or we establish beliefs. These may be intricate or very simple. They may be conscious or unconscious. We then apply the theories, frameworks, models or beliefs in a new situation that then leads to a new experience and so the cycle continues.

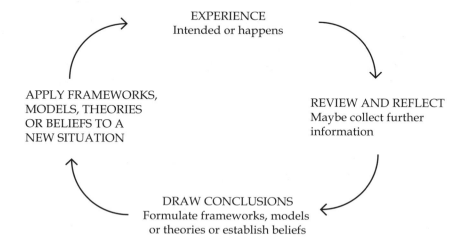

Figure 7.2   The learning cycle

Honey and Mumford have discovered (1992) that each of us tends to learn more effectively at one or two of the points on Kolb's learning cycle than at the others. They describe these as our preferred learning styles. They label individuals according to these preferences:

▌ *Activists* feel more comfortable learning from experience. They tend to prefer activity to reflection and are rather impatient with academic debate and theories. When they buy a new gadget they are more likely to try it out, and learn by doing, than read the book of instructions.

▌ *Reflectors* feel more comfortable learning by listening, reading or observing. They prefer to avoid learning situations where they are required to be in the limelight.

▌ *Theorists* feel more comfortable when learning by solving problems, using analytical skills and relating what is being learnt to a broader system, model, concept or theory or to the 'big picture'. They like ideas even if they do not have an immediate application. They are suspicious of checklists and assertions unsupported by research data.

▌ *Pragmatists* feel more comfortable with acquiring knowledge and skills that have an immediate practical application. They like tips that can be put into effect. They tend to be less interested in analysis and theories. Checklists appeal to them

You can get a pretty good idea of your team members' preferred learning styles by observation and discussion with them during coaching sessions. If there is a need to acquire or develop knowledge and skills quickly then it makes sense to identify a learning activity that matches the preferred style. On the other hand, if you are concerned with someone's longer-term career development you might decide, between you, that it makes more sense to select a learning activity that matches a weaker style. For example, although we can all acquire the basic knowledge of how to make an effective presentation from a book, we are unlikely to be very good at it unless we practise and receive feedback. The ambitious 'reflector' might not be comfortable with making a presentation. Nevertheless it might be a crucial experience if it is something that the person would be expected to do later on when in a more senior position within the firm.

Here are some suggestions to help you when planning learning events:

▌ *Activists learn best when:*
  - they have the opportunity to learn by doing, by for instance chairing a meeting, making a sales pitch or delivering a seminar;

- they participate in brainstorming sessions;
- they are thrown in at the deep end with a task and are given the opportunity to fathom out the answer for themselves.

▌ *Reflectors learn best when:*
- they can observe others at work, for instance by shadowing an expert or taking a back seat at a meeting;
- reading books;
- surfing the net;
- watching videos;
- they have time to think before acting, by for example having the opportunity to read a brief giving background data beforehand;
- they have an opportunity, with a coach, to review what has happened and what has been learnt.

▌ *Theorists learn best when:*
- they have the opportunity to explore methodically the links between ideas and events;
- they can relate the learning to a system, model, concept or theory;
- they have an opportunity to question and probe methodologies, by for instance checking papers for inconsistencies or taking part in question-and-answer sessions;
- they are stretched intellectually, for example by analysing complicated data or by teaching intelligent people who ask searching questions;
- they undertake a tough research project;
- they solve problems requiring rigorous analysis and logical thought.

▌ *Pragmatists learn best when:*
- there is an obvious link between the subject matter and tasks that have to be undertaken;
- they receive tips, techniques and checklists for doing things with practical benefits, such as how to use time effectively, how to draft a document and how to deal with difficult people;
- they have the chance to practise techniques, in simulated conditions, with feedback from a skilled performer and from video recordings. Examples include doing an interview, making a presentation and conducting a negotiation;
- there is an early opportunity to implement what has been learnt;
- they can draw up a list of action points;
- learning is rooted in real issues or problems.

Our understanding of the different ways that people learn helps us, and those whom we coach, to choose appropriate vehicles for further learning. In organizational life, training courses, seminars or workshops are perhaps the more common ways of meeting learning needs. Sometimes they are public and sometimes tailored specifically to the firm's requirements. Our understanding of learning preferences helps us to judge the effectiveness of these formal training courses. Given that any course or seminar is almost certain to include participants with each of the preferred learning styles, we need to ask ourselves if there is a good mix of learning events sufficient to satisfy all needs. Although there are other important factors to consider, the better courses and tutors are likely to offer a range of experiences appropriate to each of the preferred styles of learning.

The team leader, as coach, can play a useful role in debriefing people who have attended courses and seminars. When I was a young manager returning from my first external training programme, my boss said, 'Well, have you enjoyed yourself?' I nodded. He went on, 'Good, then that's over and done with; now back to work'. Clearly that wasn't the ideal way to debrief. The more helpful questions to ask would have been 'What have you learnt?' and 'What are you going to do as a result?' Good coaches follow up, subsequently, by discussing what has happened and helping with further learning.

There are a number of other useful learning assignments that can be undertaken in-house. In each case a good role for the coach is to help the learner to plan and then periodically to discuss progress and implementation. Among the more common possibilities are reading, use of software (especially if it is interactive), research projects, shadowing credible performers, secondments, short- or long-term membership of firm-wide project teams, and scheduled experience in new work activities.

The use of learning sets is a more recent innovation. They are usually made available for those with leadership responsibilities but can be extended to others. The idea is to bring together a group of, say, six people from different parts of the firm or from different firms. They meet for a day, every two months or so, usually with a facilitator who manages the process and makes his or her own contribution to the proceedings. There is no formal agenda. Individuals take turns to raise issues of current concern. They may relate to any aspect of work, career aspirations, life-and-work balance and so on. The other participants contribute to the learning process first by asking questions to get to the nub of the issue and, secondly, through further questioning and the sharing of thoughts and experiences, to identify possible solutions. The benefits are threefold. Problem owners usually get some insights that help them to take action.

The other participants learn, in general terms, about the handling of specific issues that they may not have previously experienced. Everyone has the opportunity to hone their listening and questioning skills. In one sense a learning set is an exercise in collective coaching. It is a good way, apart from the other benefits, for team leaders to develop their coaching skills.

GIVE AND RECEIVE FEEDBACK

The motivational benefits of positive feedback were explored in Chapter 6. Acknowledging and recognizing good performance is a strong reinforcement of behaviour and encourages people to continue to strive for first-class results. There are also occasions, of course, when it is necessary to give feedback about the things that people don't do so well so that they can learn and put matters right. It is a difficult art. Some team leaders avoid it. Others give feedback but insensitively. Relatively few handle it well. Some people pride themselves on being straight and to the point. But repeated blows delivered in the name of honesty and directness are usually damaging. There are some useful guidelines for giving feedback to help people to improve in a way that both the giver and recipient find comfortable, acceptable and effective:

▌ State the purpose of the feedback so that the recipient understands your intentions.

▌ Stick to the facts and avoid emotive words. It is hardly surprising that Jack responds defensively if he is told that he is obnoxious, rude and arrogant. Although far from easy for him, he is more likely to cope if he learns that 'in this morning's meeting he rejected every idea offered by others in a peremptory fashion and that he interrupted on at least a dozen occasions'.

▌ Talk about behaviour rather than personality. People can change their behaviour but not their personalities. In any case, commenting adversely about an individual's personality traits usually and understandably leads to defensiveness.

▌ Be specific rather than general. There is not much that Jean can do if she is told that she has an attitude problem. It is more helpful for her to learn that she responded to the last three requests for urgent information with the comment, 'I am up to my ears with work. I will deal with it when I have finished everything else. It has to go to the bottom of the pile.' If she is then helped to think through how to prioritize her work then she may change.

▌ Avoid using words like 'always' and 'never' when describing some-one's behaviour. They usually irritate and cause people to be defensive. In any event they are almost invariably untrue.

▌ Give feedback at the earliest opportunity after the event, subject to the recipient's readiness to hear it.

▌ Refer to the effects of the behaviour on you. A comment along the lines of 'When you interrupt me I lose my train of thought' gives a clear indication to Laurence about the effect of his behaviour on you. When the feedback is put into context in this way it is more readily believed and the recipient is more likely to do something about it.

▌ Check for understanding. We spend our lives being misunderstood. Feedback is a sensitive matter so it is important to check. Ask Sarah how she interprets your comments. You can then assess whether her version is the one that you intended.

▌ Think about your motives for giving feedback. Are you sure that you are giving feedback to help the recipient to change rather than to get things off your chest?

▌ Beware of playing the amateur psychologist. Stick to facts and avoid theorizing about possible, but unlikely, deep-seated early-life causes of behaviour.

▌ Agree on the action to be taken. If appropriate offer your help.

Since giving and receiving feedback is a tough call for both of you, finish by showing your appreciation of the recipient for being willing to discuss the issue and for being prepared to take some action.

Feedback doesn't always work. Most of us, however, although we may find it uncomfortable and it may come as a surprise to us, are willing to change when we learn about the damaging effects of our behaviour. But this is only true if the feedback is given in a constructive and sensitive fashion. If the guidelines are followed then recipients of feedback are less likely to react defensively.

Good leaders create a climate that encourages their team members to seek feedback. It is more effective when the recipient feels that she or he needs and is willing to receive it. Once again mutual trust and leadership by example are the building blocks. Trust has to be there before people will readily ask for feedback. Leadership by example, in this sense, means that the team leader not only shows a clear willingness to receive feedback from colleagues but also goes out of his or her way to seek it. Team members who see the leader behaving in this fashion are more likely to be prepared to accept feedback and act on it.

ENCOURAGE TEAM MEMBERS TO COACH WELL

In many professional service teams it is not only the team leaders who coach. Other senior colleagues frequently supervise the work of trainees and less experienced people. Some coaches, or supervisors as they are called in some professions, do an excellent job. They have a talent for the task and deploy first-class skills. They may have learnt from their own experiences of having been coached. However, many of them are not naturals. It is part of the team leader's job, in my view, to ensure that they receive some help with the skills needed. This may come from the team leader personally or from elsewhere. It doesn't matter as long as it happens.

I am often struck by the wealth of talent and experience in a typical professional service team that is not shared with colleagues. There are time pressures, of course, which force professionals to concentrate on the coalface job. It is understandable. But it is not usually as simple as that. The belief that it is not really their job to help others is still surprisingly prevalent among some types of professional worker. Perhaps it is rooted in the historic preference, prevalent in some professions, for working alone, sticking to one's expertise and keeping clients to oneself. Perhaps the idea of professional skills providing an individual competitive advantage is a contributory factor. Most professional service firms, these days, extol the virtues of teamwork. Part of good teamwork is sharing knowledge, skills and experience. A good way to promote this is to encourage team members to act as sounding boards for their colleagues and to provide help and guidance when requested. In other words, in an effective team, coaching is everybody's business. In those firms that go beyond lip service, and make it happen, it is the team leaders who pave the way.

8

Teamwork: Getting the best out of people working together

> *The jazz greats including John Coltrane, Charlie Parker and Louis Armstrong also understood collaboration; they knew that a great jazz performance requires more than individual excellence. Members of their combos listened carefully to the others and played in a tightly integrated and collaborative group environment. Not only did they work collaboratively, but they distinguished their performance by being creative, while at the same time playing within the structure of the song or tune.*
>
> — (Terrell Stafford)

Ask a managing partner or other senior leader of professionals if good teamwork is necessary and you will invariably get a positive response. It will probably be along the lines of, 'A well-led and coordinated team, working together to achieve agreed objectives, produces better results than a collection of individuals accountable only for their own performance.' It sounds trite. It is easy to say but getting it to happen is difficult enough in any organization. With professionals who often prefer to work alone and to be responsible purely for their own efforts it is especially tricky.

Nigel Knowles, Managing Partner at DLA, puts the problem in a nutshell:

> In my experience many lawyers are insecure. They are happiest when working quietly in their silos doing their own specialized professional work. They are nervous about stepping out of their comfort zones. So it is quite hard to get them to work well in teams. They don't always find it easy to contribute to business planning; to support each other; to pass on their skills; to participate in business decision making; to work together on major professional matters; and to pitch, as part of a team, for big new assignments.
>
> Team leaders have to devote a lot of effort, therefore, to promoting good teamwork. Encouraging people to participate in decision making, giving everyone a chance to influence outcomes, lots of oral communication and above all leading by example are crucial. Team leaders need to be very skilful at running meetings. It is not readily given to everyone but people can learn. Getting a group to work well as a team requires lots of drive and enthusiasm but above all belief in what is being done and how it can be done. Belief, when it is there, shines through. It is critical. This does not mean that the team leader necessarily has to be noisy about it. For lots of team leaders drive and belief shine through in a quiet way.

The benefits that accrue to a group of professionals working well together as a team include:

- a greater capacity to cope with complicated professional matters by being able to utilize a wider but related range of experience and talent;

- better professional and business decisions arising from collective rather than individual wisdom – several heads are better than one;

- more and better ideas for improving service quality, marketing, skill development, data banks, systems and processes;

- better marketing by harnessing the different talents of individuals, for example some make formal sales presentations, others write articles, one or two run seminars and a few network among potential clients;

- improved client service by always having people available to deal with queries and respond to requests;

- easier sharing of knowledge, skills and experience;

▌ better development of trainees and younger professionals through shared work scheduling and coaching;

▌ improved reputation in the marketplace by being able to promote a strong and talented team working together;

▌ stronger support of colleagues for each other when needed;

▌ improved ability to attract talented professionals from outside by virtue of having a strong and successful team profile in the recruitment marketplace.

There can be little doubt about the benefits of having strong and effective teams. The important thing is how to bring them into effect. The rest of this chapter is devoted to looking at some useful ways of achieving this. A good starting point is to get your team to make an assessment of how well it is working and how to bring about improvements.

HOLD TEAM DISCUSSIONS ON HOW WELL THE TEAM IS WORKING

The box 'Questions about team working' provides a list of questions about the effectiveness of teams. How many of the questions can you and your team members answer with a yes? How many can you answer not only with a yes but also with the observation that you do it really well?

QUESTIONS ABOUT TEAM WORKING

▐ Does your team have a few clear objectives?

▐ Do all team members, including the support people, have opportunities to contribute to objective setting?

▐ Is there support for each other in tough times?

▐ Is there an open expression of true beliefs and opinions rather than holding back or resorting to euphemisms?

▌ Are conflicts aired and solved?

▌ Is there a regular review of team performance for learning rather than blaming?

▌ Is there a high level of trust among team members?

▌ Are communications between team members good?

▌ Are communications with others outside the team good?

▌ Is sufficient time given to planning the future?

▌ Are team meetings both time efficient and genuinely open?

▌ Are all team members listened to rather than just the strong personalities?

▌ Do team members help each other to develop skills?

▌ Are team members good at generating ideas when together?

▌ Do team members strive to reach a genuine consensus before taking action?

▌ Does the team avoid 'groupthink' during team discussions? ('Groupthink' is a mode of thinking that people engage in when their striving for unanimity overrides their motivation to appraise options, sufficiently and realistically, before deciding what to do.)

▌ Do team members give each other honest feedback?

▌ Is there a broad mix of skills and personal attributes?

▌ Do team members accept collective responsibility for decisions? (Collective responsibility is accepting the team's decision and giving full support to its implementation even if there were reservations during the discussion and decision-making stages.)

Most of the questions posed in the box are easily understood. There may be some uncertainty about consensus, 'groupthink' and collective responsibility. These concepts are explored more fully a little later.

When teams meet together it is usually so that the participants can tackle issues that relate to their professional work or business matters that they believe require collective attention. It is relatively rare to find professional service team colleagues meeting to reflect on how well they work together. If you believe that there is a strong link between the means and the achievements of collaborative effort then it makes sense, from time to time, to assess teamworking processes. A good starting point is for team members to provide their individual responses to questions like those posed in the box. The answers can be discussed and if there is a good measure of agreement on the need for improvements then the team can produce some simple action points for putting things right. After three months or so the team can return to the questions and check that the intended changes have been brought into effect. Periodic assessments of how well the team members are working together are a good way of improving team performance. They need not take up much time. Yet the small investment of effort involved often pays off handsomely not only in more harmonious working relationships but also in hard business results.

STRIVE FOR A GENUINE CONSENSUS, AVOID GROUPTHINK AND ESTABLISH COLLECTIVE RESPONSIBILITY

When a team comes together to make a collective decision on a professional or business matter it is very easy for the leader to fall into the temptation of sounding out views around the table and then calling for a vote. The attraction is speed and saving time. However, there are dangers. Voting splits the team into winners and losers. The losers may then be less dedicated to implementing the decisions with enthusiasm. Many successful leaders try a different route. They attempt to achieve a consensus or, in other words, a meeting of minds. If everyone can say, in effect, 'I don't agree with every detail but I accept the broad thrust of the decision' then a consensus has been achieved. Although it may take longer to arrive at, a decision based on consensus has two advantages. First, if the team explores options fully and then reaches a consensus it will usually produce a better decision. Secondly, if there is a genuine consensus then each team member will feel more committed to turning the decision into action.

Some teams, in striving for a consensus, fall instead into the trap of 'groupthink'. A US political scientist, Irving L Janis, coined this rather inelegant word. It is useful shorthand for a mode of thinking, which people engage in during discussions, when their striving for unanimity overrides their motivation to appraise options, sufficiently and realistically, before deciding what to do. Janis showed in his book, *Groupthink: Psychological studies of policy decisions and fiascoes* (1982), that several US foreign policy blunders in the second half of the 20th century were the result of the psychological drive for unanimity at any cost, the suppression of disagreement and the failure to appraise options thoroughly. Groupthink is always a risk in collective decision making and occurs just as readily in business teams as within government.

Some of the more common symptoms of groupthink are:

- There are illusions of unanimity. For instance, assumptions such as 'silence means consent' are made.

- There is direct pressure on team members who express arguments against the prevailing view. Inferences of lack of loyalty are common.

- Individuals hold back from speaking against the majority view because they fear ridicule or they worry about wasting the team's time.

- Illusions of invulnerability exist because the team has been very successful in the past.

- There is a strong belief in the inherent morality of the team. Paradoxically this inclines team members to ignore the ethical consequences of their current decisions.

- Problems or obstacles are explained away. Such rationalization may lead to a failure to analyse information objectively.

- Some individuals prevent the team from hearing adverse information that might violate a shared complacency about the justification of decisions.

The more usual causes of groupthink are:

- The team is a highly cohesive and amiable group with strong *esprit de corps*. (Of course cohesion is not in itself bad, quite the contrary, but there are risks.)

- The team leader and other senior figures, or strong personalities, dominate and also lack impartiality.

- The team does not have methodical and objective ways of working.

▌ The team is rather insulated and not sufficiently open to external influences and thinking.

▌ The team members all share the same values and beliefs. (In many respects that is a good thing but as with all strengths there is also an underlying weakness.)

▌ The importance of the decision, its complexity and tight deadlines all put team members under great pressure.

Typical consequences of groupthink are:

▌ Objectives are not fully understood.

▌ The assessment of options is superficial.

▌ The risks of the preferred course of action are not examined thoroughly.

▌ Options that may have been rejected previously on inadequate grounds are not reappraised.

▌ Sufficient high-quality information to assist with objective analysis is not obtained.

▌ Too little time is spent on how the chosen decision might be opposed, damaged, sabotaged or hindered by inertia. As a result, contingency plans are not prepared.

▌ There is a selective bias in evaluating data. It often takes the form of accepting too readily those facts and opinions that support the initially preferred course of action and rejecting those that do not.

The difficult trick for team leaders is to work towards consensus and, at the same time, prevent 'groupthink'. If 'groupthink' occurs then a consensus is apparent rather than real. Allowing sufficient time to deliberate on serious decisions is a prerequisite. Effective leaders encourage differences of opinions and make a point of urging their teams to explore options fully before deciding what to do.

I have noticed that, even if they don't always succeed, good professional service leaders strive for a genuine consensus among team members. There is a world of difference between working for a consensus, and sometimes failing and having finally to resort to a vote, and taking the more cavalier approach of keeping the discussion brief and calling for a vote too early. The former is hard work but usually results in a good decision and team member commitment. The latter is easy but frequently less effective. With luck the decision might be right but enthusiastic implementation by those who voted against is far from guaranteed.

The notion of collective responsibility has its roots in an old convention of the unwritten British constitution. Collective cabinet responsibility implies that decisions freely arrived at should always be loyally supported afterwards by the ministers. Some authorities argue that this doctrine no longer applies in government. Whether that is true or not there is a great deal to be said for its application in professional service teams. Smooth and speedy execution is much easier to achieve if team members give full support afterwards for decisions in which they have had a say. It is both obvious and interesting to note that collective responsibility is much easier to achieve when decisions are based on a consensus rather than a vote. If you back the decision then it is much easier to give enthusiastic support to its implementation.

At PricewaterhouseCoopers the notions of consensus and collective responsibility are alive and well. Richard Sexton, partner in charge of the London assurance practice, says:

> I try to achieve a consensus so that there is broad agreement on what we want to do. The idea is for everybody to be able to live comfortably with the decision, even if they do not agree with every last detail. It is then much easier for everyone to accept collective responsibility. Getting consensus is sometimes a struggle, especially when it involves people themselves having to change. It is much easier to achieve it when we are dealing with structures, procedures and processes. But even where it is difficult, it is right to work for it.

Richard Sexton's colleague Richard Collier-Keywood expresses an interesting view about collective responsibility and leadership:

> In this business, in my view, the best leaders are also the best followers. Take collective responsibility: we regard this as being very important. Once decisions have been taken everyone is expected to back them and neither criticize them to others nor sabotage them. That is easy to say but not always easy to do. I have to work as a team member at one level and I have my own team at another. If I accept collective responsibility as a team member, which I do, then this becomes apparent to the people in my own team. That is leadership by example and it is the best way to get the message home.

However, for teams of intelligent and well-motivated people to make good decisions they need to be skilfully led. Here are some tips to help team leaders to achieve high-quality decisions based on genuine consensus:

▌ Encourage disagreement and the constructive conflict of ideas, but not personalities, in the early stages of the discussion.

▌ As team leader, avoid stating your opinions early in the discussion so that others are not discouraged from giving their views. Invite the quieter members of the team to give their opinions.

▌ Encourage the team to identify options and analyse the pros and cons of each. Bear in mind the importance of weighing some pros and cons more heavily than others.

▌ If the team reaches deadlock, try to resolve the problem by separating facts from beliefs. It often works.

▌ Steer the team towards a conclusion only after everybody has had an opportunity to contribute and after the pros and cons of each option have been assessed.

Here is a final word about using the team to make collective decisions on the more important business and professional matters. Bringing the team members together for this purpose and making the effort to achieve a genuine consensus and to avoid 'groupthink' has two benefits. The higher-quality decisions that generally result and the commitment to their achievement have already been noted. There is also a significant by-product. Team spirit is fostered, individuals value each other's contributions and people improve their skills in working together.

USE THE TEAM TO GENERATE AND EVALUATE IDEAS

Professional service teams need to develop new services from time to time; exploit new markets; develop their marketing effectiveness; look for ways to enhance client care; introduce new systems and processes to increase productivity; and change working practices to improve performance. Innovations are necessary for firms to remain relevant and competitive. A continuing stream of ideas is a prerequisite. Good leaders encourage their colleagues to offer ideas individually but there is also merit in using the team, when together, for this purpose. When teams brainstorm ideas, assuming that the process is facilitated effectively, people spark each other off and build on the ideas of their colleagues. There is usually some useful synergy therefore from the team effort.

Here are examples of issues for which your team could generate ideas. You will think of many others:

▌ What new services could we offer to existing and prospective clients?

▌ In which business sectors or geographical areas, where we do not currently work, could we seek new clients?

▌ In what new ways could we market our services?

▌ How can we improve our recruitment so that we attract more talented people?

▌ What changes in working practices would enhance profitability?

▌ What changes in working practices would enhance cash flow?

▌ How can we get our existing clients to refer us to other clients?

▌ What new skills do we need to develop to improve our performance?

▌ How can we reduce bureaucracy and red tape?

▌ How can we improve our communications with other parts of the business?

There are several techniques that you can use to generate ideas. If you have never done it before it is probably best to start with a simple brainstorming exercise. You or one of your team colleagues will need to facilitate the discussion and agree with everyone that some basic guidelines be followed. They are usually along the lines of those recommended originally by Alex Osborn in his book *Applied Imagination: The principles and procedures of creative thinking* (1953). They first appeared in the 1950s but have stood the test of time. Osborn believed that people are not as creative as they might be because they 'drive with the brake on'. Too often they try to be creative and critical at the same time. He famously said, 'It is a little like trying to get hot and cold water out of the same faucet at the same time: the ideas may not be hot enough, the evaluation of them not cold or objective enough. The results will be tepid.' He recommended that idea generation and idea evaluation should be kept separate from each other. The first step should be to produce ideas. Judging them should be deferred until a later stage. He derived his thinking from Hindu teachers working with religious groups in India. During the process of Prai-Bashana (Prai means 'outside yourself' and Bashana means 'question'), ideas were brought out but there was no discussion and no criticism. The groups met again later to debate and assess the ideas.

Useful guidelines for the idea generation phase are:

▌ Display a statement of the issue or problem for which ideas are required where everyone can see it.

▌ Ask the participants to suspend judgement outwardly but also, if possible, within the mind. Criticism kills creativity. Remind your colleagues of the common response to new ideas, which is to find several reasons why they won't work. The self-discipline involved in suspending judgement, both internally and externally, is difficult at first, especially for those professionals who use analytical and critical skills in their jobs.

▌ Invite everyone to 'freewheel' and think laterally. Suggest that they say everything that comes to mind. Ideas can be serious, eccentric, funny, practical or half-baked. It doesn't matter. Remember the philosopher Alfred White's comment, 'There is a certain amount of foolishness in any idea when it is first produced'. All new ideas go against the existing grain. In any case wild ideas can be tamed afterwards. There is not much that can be done with the mundane. Many people find this tricky at first. Most of us are used to thinking carefully before speaking in meetings. Like most things it becomes easier with practice.

▌ Encourage colleagues to build on each other's ideas. Creativity tends to be greatest when people let their minds go with the flow of ideas rather than flying off in different directions. Try to get a large number of ideas recorded before bringing the brainstorming session to a close. The more ideas there are, the greater the chance, generally speaking, of finding something of value.

▌ The facilitator (team leader or colleague) manages the process. All ideas are written down on flip charts and posted around the room or displayed on a large screen with the use of a laptop computer. It is the facilitator's job to discourage judging and to stop discussions developing, although some clarification can be helpful. A good facilitator also monitors the level of energy and calls for a break if the batteries need to be recharged. It is good practice to give everyone a few minutes to write ideas down before the brainstorming begins. Everyone, including the more reserved participants, then has something to contribute. One method is then to go round the table asking each person to contribute one idea at a time until all have been revealed. Another is to invite people to call ideas out at random but no more than one idea at a time. Building on the ideas of others is encouraged.

Brainstorming, because it requires people to behave differently from usual, is best undertaken in a meeting set up primarily for the purpose. Relaxed surroundings can be beneficial. Two or three, but not six or seven, glasses of wine generally help. Successful sessions are often preceded by a warm-up light-hearted brainstorm for 5 or 10 minutes. The team can be invited to generate ideas for 'new uses for empty shoe polish tins' or 'new uses for discarded red telephone booths', for instance. These sessions produce plenty of humour, relax the participants and get everyone in a more creative frame of mind. It is not a bad idea to put the fool's cap on once in a while. It is even a better idea to keep it on for the serious brainstorming session that follows. After all, the fool's job is to shake the habits, rules and conventions that keep us thinking in the old ways and keep us travelling in the old ruts. There are other ways of using the team to generate ideas. Here are a few of them:

▌ Get your team members to fashion an analogy for a problem requiring ideas. For instance, they might suggest 'how to start a revolution' for 'how to get lawyers to bill early rather than late'. They might recommend 'how to create a beautiful flower arrangement' for 'how to improve the coordination of work between team members'. Another possibility would be 'how to do good stand-up comedy' for 'how to make an effective formal sales pitch'. The further away the analogy is from the real issue, in terms of its context, so much the better.

Having agreed on an analogy the team then lists as many reasons as possible why the fictitious problem is difficult to solve. In the case of 'how to create a beautiful flower arrangement', these might include no water; all of the flowers are the same colour; the flower arranger is clumsy; it is winter; and the vase is too big. It is usually possible to invent 30 or 40 causes, crazy as well as serious, by brainstorming. The next stage is to formulate one or two solutions for each. These may be serious, practical, amusing, eccentric or plain daft. Finally, the solutions to the analogous problem are then applied to the original real issue with the aim of obtaining insights rather than literal applications. People who use the analogy technique generally say that they find it easier to think laterally. They feel less constrained by the problem and are frequently able to produce rather more novel solutions.

▌ Get your team to seek inspirations from other contexts. We all know that many successful inventions have their sources in the natural world. George Mistral walked his dog in the foothills of the Swiss Alps. He found burrs of the burdock weed stuck to his trousers and to the dog. He examined them under a microscope and discovered a fine mesh of tiny hooks that provided adhesion. It was a small jump in imagination for him to create the product we all know as Velcro.

The dragonfly for reasons of security is able to look in all directions. The structure of its eye provided the inspiration for the design of the cockpit of the spotter plane that allows the pilot and passengers to look upwards, downwards and through a circle. Serendipity under-pinned the inspirations for these inventions. However, you and your team can deliberately seek inspiration from other contexts. If you need fresh ideas, for instance, on how to raise morale or improve service quality, why not ask each member of the team to spend some time in a library looking at book titles, in a museum looking at the exhibits or in a gallery looking at the paintings? Alternatively you could ask them to look through an atlas, study pictures in a magazine or read news-paper headlines. In each case the purpose is to search for and record anything that relates to or sheds fresh light on the problem for which ideas are required. Afterwards bring your team together and invite them in turn to describe what they found and explain how it relates to the question that you are seeking to answer. Any fresh ideas stimulated by these comments can be shared. Discussions, which need not take too long, often throw up fresh and interesting answers.

▌ Identify a problem or issue for which ideas are needed. Then ask each member of your team to think about an experience from outside current work that might indirectly have a bearing on the problem and that might provide an insight into solving it. The experience could be from, for instance, pastimes, sports, previous jobs, school or college days, time in the armed services or voluntary work. Ask your colleagues in turn to tell their stories. Discuss the experiences and try to identify how the insights that emerge help the team to resolve the problem or satisfy the issue for which ideas are required.

Jonathan Hood, a partner at law firm Thomas Eggar, describes idea generation in his firm:

> Brainstorming is deceptively simple. The usual idea is for people to put their heads together to see if, through suitably animated discussion, useful ideas emerge. Practice is often different. Some individuals dominate in meetings and inhibit the more reticent to come forward. There are in-built restrictions such as deference, shyness, reluctance to have an idea laughed at, fear of offending and so on. Exhortations to 'think out of the box' do nothing to remove the inherent problem.
>
> One technique however which my firm has employed with success in trying to tackle such perennial problems as the development of marketing ideas, a topic which tends to be a spectacular turn off for many lawyers, is formal brainstorming which requires the observance of some specific guidelines. There are many versions. The one we have employed involves splitting a group into sub teams. Large numbers assist. Each team is asked to produce say five ideas. This starts the process off. These ideas are then written on large sheets of paper and displayed on a wall. Then everyone simply wanders around looking at the ideas. The teams then reassemble and discuss whether any of the ideas displayed have stimulated any further ideas. If so those are then in turn posted up. During this process everyone is encouraged to avoid being critical. Quite the contrary, people are invited to look for the possibilities. Emphasis is placed on thinking laterally and on building on each other's ideas.
>
> By this time the individual and collective wells of invention will have been plumbed. It is often the case that an idea, however bizarre, can trigger off a train of thought that may itself prove interesting. Nobody has been exposed to ridicule for the more extraordinary suggestions and nobody claims ownership of any one thought. From this point on discussion can then commence on the ideas that have struck a general chord and a shortlist of attractive ideas can be produced.
>
> Another, and very useful approach, particularly with problems that are politically sensitive or that have in the past proved intractable, is to get the participants to come up with an analogy

for the issue. Instead of addressing the actual problem, time is spent brainstorming solutions to the analogous problem. For example an analogy for opening a new office in an area with no clients might be creating a wildlife park in a country where none exists currently. The solutions to the analogous problem are then reviewed to identify insights into solving the real issue. The more offbeat the analogy then the more novel and startling, and innovative, the ideas tend to be.

Not surprisingly advertising agencies make a habit of getting people together to produce ideas. They are good at it. According to Ian Pearman, Account Director at Abbott Mead Vickers, the tougher job for their teams comes at the evaluation stage:

> Of course, we get our teams together to come up with ideas. That is no problem. We are good at ideas. Our problem is to decide what to do with the ideas. We don't need to be told to think outside the box; we do that all of the time. Getting the issues back inside the box, properly defining and distilling a problem and its potential solution, is the challenge for us. It's a bit like nailing jelly to the wall.

After the brainstorming or other idea generation session, it is helpful to have a period for reflection, an incubation phase, before moving on to the evaluation process. Giving people the opportunity to sleep on the ideas and return to them for evaluation purposes in a day or two's time can be fruitful. There is no hard-and-fast way to evaluate ideas. One method is to ask the team to select all of the interesting ideas. If an idea is exciting but impractical you can run another brainstorming session devoted to turning the idea into a practical proposition. Another way of screening ideas is to assess them in terms of their attractiveness, for example originality, simplicity and elegance and their compatibility with, for instance, objectives and resources.

You may finish up with two or three ideas that can be implemented immediately. Some ideas will require personal action by all team members and they will become part of a new way of working. Volunteers, on behalf of the team, may implement others. It is important to agree target dates for delivery. There will be other ideas that need to be honed or refined before they can be put into effect. Sometimes research may be necessary or the ideas may need to be sold to people elsewhere in the firm. Again volunteers can be invited to take on these commitments.

It is important that people do not take on more than they can chew. After an idea generation and evaluation session, team members are often fired up and enthusiastic. It is very much the team leader's job to ensure that the commitments and target dates are realistic. After all, this work is additional to the regular fee-earning or other activities that team colleagues are involved in. I have noticed, time and time again, that when there is a failure to turn good ideas into action it is because the individuals involved have committed themselves to doing too much in too short a period of time. A good motto for team members is: 'Don't commit if you believe you can't do it but if you do commit then you must do it.'

ENCOURAGE TEAM MEMBERS TO HELP EACH OTHER TO DEVELOP SKILLS

Typically professional service teams contain a huge amount and variety of talent and experience. Often it is utilized in a rather piecemeal fashion. In the good teams, time is put aside on a regular basis so that best practice can be shared. Investment in skill development, in this way, really does bring to life the old clichés 'Our people are our most important asset' and 'Our people are our only asset'. There are a few straightforward ways for you to help your team colleagues to share knowledge and help each other to build skills:

▌ Arrange for team members to pass on new professional or business knowledge that they have acquired during the last two or three months and that is likely to be of value to their colleagues. Basic information can be passed on in writing but in most cases knowledge is best shared, collectively, with colleagues, with opportunities for questions and discussion.

▌ Arrange for those with exceptional skills to demonstrate them to their colleagues. Apart from specific professional and technical skills, examples include making sales presentations at tenders, conducting negotiations, handling difficult clients, conducting selection interviews, chairing meetings and undertaking coaching. Some of these activities might involve some simple practical exercises.

▌ Encourage team colleagues to use each other as sounding boards and coaches.

▌ Encourage team members to shadow colleagues with strong skills in such activities as client relations, networking, negotiating, conducting information-gathering interviews and making presentations. Observing the effective use of skills followed by a discussion and questions is a particularly useful way for people to learn. Whilst it is common enough in the professions for trainees to develop their skills by shadowing skilful performers there is a lot to be said for extending the practice to team colleagues generally.

▌ Invite individuals to research professional or business topics that will be of value to the team as a whole, and arrange for them to present and discuss their findings.

Sharing the results of learning and helping each other to develop skills are not only intrinsically useful and cost effective but they also help to underpin good teamwork generally. They also reinforce the notion of lifelong learning in an increasingly volatile and complicated business world.

REMIND THE TEAM THAT IT IS STILL A TEAM WHEN IT IS APART

Teams are apart for much more time than they are together. Most professionals spend large amounts of their time writing, reading, calculating, designing, researching and in meetings with clients. Much of the time is spent on technical or professional matters and some on business tasks. It is part of the leader's job to create a climate where team members can enjoy their autonomy and yet be sufficiently disciplined and willing to be team players. Keeping their colleagues informed on matters that are important to them is a good example. The agreement of ground rules of the sort described in Chapter 4 provides a good basis for this to happen. But even with ground rules, good leaders still keep an eye on what is happening. They monitor behaviour without being too intrusive and gently remind people about the agreed norms of behaviour. It is much easier to remind them when they have agreed to them in the first place.

These are some of the things that good team players do as a matter of routine:

▌ Provide information quickly to their colleagues when it is requested.

▌ Take the initiative to keep colleagues informed on matters that they think are important to them.

▌ Help colleagues to solve problems when requested.

▌ Lend a hand when colleagues have too much to do.

▌ Willingly intercept phone calls for colleagues who are away from their desks or who need uninterrupted time for concentrated effort.

▌ Willingly act as sounding boards for colleagues wanting to check out planned ways of proceeding.

▌ Fulfil all of their commitments rather than just their professional or fee-earning ones.

▌ Flag up impending crises or major problems in good time.

▌ Remind their colleagues of the team's ground rules when they are not being observed.

▌ Act as ambassadors for the team and its work.

▌ Willingly step in on behalf of colleagues who are absent if the situation demands.

There is a final and very important point for team leaders to bear in mind. Using teams constructively has great merit. Successful leaders of professionals recognize this. We have also noted that they also have to have the ability to balance the needs of the team and the needs of its individuals. Team members need the authority and freedom to get on with their day-to-day work. Good leaders are adept at creating the space for this to happen but within the context of clear and agreed objectives and norms of behaviour. If the context is right then good performance usually follows. If there is no proper framework within which people can act effectively then, however talented they are, anarchy is more likely to result. The challenge for team leaders is to get the best out of the team, as a whole, whilst at the same time enabling each individual member to excel.

9

Difficulties: Resolving poor performance, interpersonal conflicts and crises

*Leadership has a harder job to do than just choosing sides;
it must bring sides together.*

— (Jesse Jackson)

*The ultimate measure of a man is not where he stands
in moments of comfort and convenience but where he stands
at times of challenge and controversy.*

— (Martin Luther King)

The acid test of outstanding leadership is to take the right action when things are going wrong. Team leaders sooner or later face serious problems. The more common are:

█ significant underperformance;

█ outstanding professional performers who refuse to be team players;

█ interpersonal disagreements between two or more team colleagues;

▌ crises such as losing a major client, a significant business downturn, a valued colleague leaving and unethical or inappropriate conduct by a member of the team.

SOLVING POOR PERFORMANCE

It is easy to turn a blind eye to poor performance until it becomes critical. Postponing action is common. Finding excuses is not unusual. Seeking rationalizations is far from rare. Not infrequently, leaders fail to face up to uncomfortable truths about the poor performance of those who are not pulling their weight. The best leaders have the courage and determination to tackle performance problems before they become very serious and impact adversely on the firm and on team colleagues. They make it clear that they want underperformance to be resolved and they offer their help. However, sometimes when they grasp the nettle they make the mistake of trying to change someone's behaviour either by appealing to reason or by issuing an ultimatum. Too often the result is failure. The mistake is to try to get people to change by using a persuasive or threatening pep talk. The reality is that change comes from within. The challenge, therefore, is to create the circumstances in which underperformers can motivate themselves. The more common reasons for poor performance appear in Table 9.1.

Table 9.1 The more common causes of poor performance

Competence	Motivation
Lack of knowledge or skills for particular tasks.	No longer finding the work interesting or challenging.
Failure to keep up to date.	Growing preference for non-work activities.
Clumsy relationship behaviour.	Fear of failure in trying something new.
	Insecurity due to merger discussions or other major changes.

Personal	Organizational/business
Loss of confidence.	Poorly led.
Major health problem.	Inadequate resources.
Family or relationship problem.	Unsupportive culture.
Alcoholism or drug addiction.	Loss of a major client.
Financial worries.	Business sector downturn.
Exhaustion.	

It is important not to jump to conclusions about the causes of poor performance. They come in many guises. Rather like medicine, the key to arriving at the right remedy is to begin with a good diagnosis. Beware of treating symptoms rather than causes. Sometimes you will have a pretty good idea especially if you make a regular habit of chatting with your colleagues. Some of the more common causes listed in Table 9.1 are easier to identify than others. Lack of knowledge or skill for particular tasks or a failure to keep up to date is not too difficult to discern. Most business influences are apparent. If the cause is personal or motivational, however, it might not be too obvious. If it turns out that you are the cause of the poor performance because you are not providing good leadership then it will probably come as an unpleasant surprise. The remedy is clearly in your own hands!

Assuming that you are not the cause of the performance problem, a good approach is to help the underperformer to come up with the right answers and then to encourage that person to take responsibility for putting things right. Here are some useful questions to help you and the individual concerned to identify the root causes of performance difficulties:

▊ What is the difference between what is being done and what should be done?

▊ What is happening that causes us to say that things are not right?

▊ Is there a knowledge or skill deficiency?

▊ Were the tasks undertaken effectively in the past?

▊ Is it punishing, psychologically, to perform as expected?

▊ Does performing appropriately get in the way of achieving other job, career or personal objectives?

▊ Are there psychological rewards for not performing in the way required? For example, is the person concerned in a comfortable rut?

▊ Does performing in the right way really matter to the person concerned?

▊ Is there a fear of change or of trying something new?

▊ Are there organizational or business obstacles to performing in the desired way?

▌ Are there conflicting demands on the time available?

▌ Are the resources, information and authority required to do the job available?

▌ Does the organizational environment or the firm's culture inhibit effective performance?

▌ Are there personal problems that may be adversely affecting performance?

When serious underperformance occurs, after a track record of success, it is unlikely to be due to a lack of knowledge or skill unless there has been a failure to keep up to date. The more likely reasons are personal, such as health or relationship problems, or motivational, such as no longer finding the work sufficiently interesting or challenging. If the cause is an organizational obstacle or a business downturn then it is quite likely that several members of the team will be affected. Whatever you suspect the reason is, the first step is to talk to the person concerned to try to find out exactly what is happening. Good leadership means not putting the problem off. It also means approaching the person and the problem, in the first instance, in a spirit of concerned enquiry. Here are some useful steps:

▌ Set up a meeting to discuss the matter. Tell your colleague that you have some concerns about how things are going but that you would like the opportunity to chat about some possible improvements. Give some notice, a day or so, for the meeting so that the person involved can give thought to the issues involved. But don't make the notice so long that it causes unnecessary anxiety.

▌ Be positive, indicate confidence in your colleague and offer help. Many performance problems can be resolved more easily when the person concerned knows that there is support rather than opposition.

▌ Get agreement that serious underperformance exists and try to identify the cause. Some people are very ready to admit that there is a difficulty and are relieved, in a way, to find that it is being addressed. Others may be defensive or may even deny that a problem exists. Sympathetic questioning, careful listening and a calm and understanding response help. It is a good idea to raise awareness by exploring the gap between what is happening and the performance expectations.

▌ Ascertain whether the poor performance is due to genuine obstacles outside the individual's control or is something that can be remedied by the person concerned. If there are organizational constraints such as inadequate resources or an unsupportive culture then it is your job as team leader to help to remove those impediments. If the problem is personal then it may be necessary to provide a breathing space for it to be remedied.

▌ For those problems that can be resolved by the individual concerned, ask questions and offer suggestions to raise awareness and generate responsibility for action. Identify a goal for improvement and explore options for achieving it. Agree on ways to make progress.

▌ Have periodic discussions to review progress. At these meetings acknowledge all improvements and achievements to build confidence and reinforce progress towards the acceptable levels of performance.

Investing time in helping people to improve is both a human and an economic answer to underperformance. Firing people and hiring replacements is a very expensive option. Those who adopt this alternative too readily seldom count the many hidden costs involved. Only consider the disciplinary route as a last resort. If all else fails then it is in the interests of the firm generally and your team specifically to warn and, if that fails to produce results, to terminate employment. Protracted serious underperformance when there is no likelihood of a remedy cannot be tolerated.

TACKLE THE RELUCTANT TEAM PLAYERS

Most firms have a handful of very competitive and professionally able people who are brilliant at generating business and delivering results. They are often very creative and instrumental in driving the firm in new and more effective directions. Usually they are able to combine these considerable talents with being effective team players. If so, the benefits to the firm can't be overestimated. Occasionally, though, however outstanding they may be as individual performers, they are hopeless at teamwork. They insist on having their own way and being strong personalities they usually succeed. They often prefer to 'walk alone' rather than participate in shared efforts such as a team marketing event. At worst they are critical, domineering, unwilling to help others, brusque and even, though charming to their own clients, rude to their colleagues. In short they behave like temperamental 'prima donnas'.

Many firms put up with this sort of behaviour because they take the view that the benefits outweigh the disadvantages. Even some of those firms that place great stress on good teamwork are prepared to make exceptions. One managing partner told me 'that whilst we believe in teamwork we occasionally have to make an exception and play to people's strengths. This means tolerating egocentric behaviour especially when the people concerned deliver good personal results.' There is a difference, I believe, between welcoming eccentricity and enjoying the creative benefits that often accompany it, and putting up with dysfunctional relationship behaviour. The price that a firm pays for letting occasional 'prima donnas' get away with irritating, annoying and frustrating their colleagues is considerable. They are failing to come into line with the firm's generally accepted ways of doing things. However talented they are personally, the effect of their behaviour on the team and the firm generally in the long run is likely to outweigh the advantages that they bring. If you want to maintain a congenial working environment, which is conducive to attracting and retaining good people, then you need to take action to deal with the reluctant team players. The suggestions in Chapter 7 on giving feedback are especially relevant. Consider using these in conjunction with the following guidelines:

▌ Describe the behaviour that is causing concern. It is particularly important to avoid commenting on personality traits. Stick to behaviour with specific examples of what you have observed. Avoid hearsay, rumours and gossip. Be frank and avoid euphemisms. Explain the adverse effect that the undesirable behaviour is having on you and your team colleagues.

▌ Try to ascertain the reasons for the unacceptable behaviour. Although it is rarely a matter of deficient communication skills or personal problems that is causing the difficulty it is nevertheless necessary to find out. More often it is a strong preference for working alone and being in total control of one's own destiny that is at the root of the problem.

▌ Help your colleague to understand that he or she will benefit from changing. Explain that people who have the respect of their colleagues are more likely to gain cooperation when it is needed. Emphasize the value for everyone that comes from willing teamwork including the sharing of knowledge, provision of ideas, better problem solving and support of each other in tough times. Stress that your colleague has a lot to offer that could lead to better results all round and rewards to follow.

▌ Ask the person concerned to suggest possible solutions. Ask questions aimed at encouraging the acceptance of responsibility to put things right. Avoid imposing your own solutions. They are likely to be resisted. Agree some small steps and goals for changing behaviour. Be prepared for small steady improvements and offer your support and encouragement. Make it very clear that you value your colleague's contributions but that you believe that things could be so very much better.

▌ Have periodic follow-up discussions to discuss progress. Reinforce changes in behaviour by acknowledging the benefits. Talk about the things that still need to be done and agree the further steps that may be taken.

▌ The greatest danger for team leaders is to indulge outstanding individual performers who are poor team players whilst at the same time taking moderate performers to task. Team members will perceive double standards. It is likely to be resented and in the worst cases lead to a lowering of morale and a consequent decline in team performance.

What happens if all of this effort fails and behaviour does not change? Managing Partner Tim Aspinall at law firm DMH is very clear about what has to be done:

> The best-performing organizations comprise individuals who share the same culture and are committed to implementing the agreed strategies. This is because everybody is pulling in the same direction and more likely to be supportive of each other. In many organizations, however, and this included DMH, there are individuals who are technically expert at what they do, often high fee earners and great work winners, but who don't fully subscribe to the culture, systems and procedures. The easy thing to do in this situation is to try and work around the individual. I have seen organizations put people like this in an office at the end of the corridor and tolerate their refusal to cooperate or, in the worst cases, their negative comments and attitudes because they are afraid to confront the problem. Although this might be seen as the easy solution it creates

much larger problems for the organization as a whole as other, more junior individuals feel that the organization tolerates behaviour like this and they ask themselves why they should conform. This leads to the organization becoming dysfunctional. I very strongly believe that individuals like this should be confronted and given the opportunity, support and guidance to change their behaviour so they become fully integrated with the organization. Ultimately though, if the individual isn't prepared to change then he or she should be asked to leave. We had to make this difficult decision at DMH. It wasn't easy but putting the organization ahead of the individual made us stronger as a firm and sent a very clear message to everyone that no one person was more important than the whole.

Cheryl Giovannoni, Chief Executive of design firm Coley Porter Bell, makes a similar observation:

Very occasionally we have people who are technically good at their work but who have the wrong attitude of mind. Perhaps they are unwilling to change in the direction that the rest of us want to go or perhaps they are not prepared to sign up to core values. We make a considerable effort to get them to modify their behaviour through formal appraisals and day-to-day coaching. Usually it works but if it doesn't then in the interests of the firm, our people and our clients we have to part company. Fortunately it is a very rare occurrence.

MANAGE INTERPERSONAL DISAGREEMENTS

Some conflict between team members is healthy and should be welcomed. If people debate matters of substance with each other and examine different points of view in a robust fashion then the team will benefit. Better solutions are likely to evolve.

However, regardless of how technically competent your people are there will inevitably be occasions when two or more of them fall out with each other or with other members of the firm. Strong negative feelings arise as a result of something said or done. Often remarks or actions are no more than thoughtless but they can still cause feelings of anger, annoyance or disappointment in others. Sometimes people deliberately 'put down' others or act selfishly with similar results. Conflicts among individuals can take several forms. The more common are avoiding talking to each other except when absolutely necessary, bickering, finding fault publicly, criticizing individuals in discussions with others and, in particularly serious cases, verbal abuse. All of these forms of conflict are unhealthy and can damage team performance.

I have noticed that many team leaders are well aware that they should tackle these disagreements before they get worse but in practice tend to avoid dealing with them. Professional life is tough and demanding, and confrontation with colleagues is often viewed as an unpleasant chore and an unrewarding hassle on top of the rest of the day's work. However, there is no question that if you turn a blind eye to serious disagreements then negative feelings are quite likely to intensify and result finally in a serious breakdown of relationships. Team morale and performance will be adversely affected.

Probably the best way for a team leader to assist in the resolution of major disagreements is to act as a mediator. There are some useful practical steps that you can take:

▌ Bring the people who are in conflict together, with you, and describe to them both the disagreement and the unproductive behaviour that you are witnessing.

▌ Make no judgements and describe the problem as being one for you, the team as a whole and the individuals concerned. Let them know that you would like this discussion to concentrate primarily on the ways in which they are relating to each other rather than on the issue that initially caused the conflict. If, between you, you are able to tackle the behaviour that is preventing your colleagues from interacting effectively then it will become much easier, subsequently, for them to resolve the original difference in a more rational manner.

▌ Ask them in turn to describe what is going on as they see it. Ask them to describe what they perceive the other person to be doing that contributes to the disagreement, and what they themselves are doing that contributes to the problem. Don't try to resolve the problem but ask questions, listen carefully and reflect back what you have heard in an effort to get to the underlying cause of the differences. Try to ascertain whether the disagreement is due to a misunderstanding about facts or information, a disagreement about how to proceed with an assignment, a disagreement about purpose or goals or a disagreement about basic beliefs or values. Try to help each person to accept some responsibility for the situation.

▪ Ask each person to summarize what the other person has said. This helps them to listen, acknowledge and understand each other's views. Ask each of them to confirm that the summary is correct or, if not, seek clarifications. Don't seek to resolve the dispute but rather listen carefully and ask questions to get as much relevant information out into the open as possible.

▪ Ask each person in turn to indicate points of agreement. It is not unusual to identify a large measure of agreement when a conflict is analysed calmly, with help from a third party, in this way.

▪ Ask each of them in turn to indicate points of disagreement and to suggest ways to resolve them. Help them, through questions, to offer some simple steps, involving give and take, to make progress.

▪ Agree a date, perhaps a month later, for the three of you to get together to review progress.

At some point it might be helpful to offer a few thoughts, to them, about how long-term effective relationships can be maintained. Roger Fisher and Scott Brown, of the Harvard Negotiating Project, provide some good, straightforward advice in their book *Getting Together: Building a relationship that gets to yes* (1989).

They suggest that for good working relationships we need not only good outcomes or results but also inner peace. For example, after a meeting with a colleague we want to feel competent, confident and content rather than uneasy, tense or angry. If we can say words to the effect 'It is always a pleasure to work with you' then this is a clear sign of positive feelings. If we don't feel positive about the last transaction then we may dread the next and have more difficulty dealing with it. They also say that we need to have an ability to handle differences constructively. We know that the other party, in any relationship, has interests that may differ from ours. We know that we have differing and changing perceptions and values. The working relationship requires accommodations that satisfy the competing interests as well as possible and in ways that are acceptable to each person. They suggest six qualities that help us to deal with such differences in a constructive manner:

▪ Try to balance reason and emotion. We cannot work well with another person when emotions overwhelm reason. We cannot make wise decisions in the middle of temper frustrations. But neither is logic alone sufficient for solving problems and building relationships.

▌ Try to understand the other person's interests and perceptions. Try to look at the world from her or his perspective. Also help the other person to understand how you see things. It will be easier to create solutions for differences if both parties understand each other even if they do not agree at first.

▌ Communicate effectively to improve understanding but also to allay suspicion. The more openly we communicate with each other the greater the chance that trust will develop.

▌ Develop trust by being reliable. Commitments entered into lightly or disregarded easily are often worse than none. Well-founded trust based on honest and reliable conduct over time can greatly enhance our ability to cope with conflicts when they arise.

▌ Be persuasive rather than coercive. It is better to try to influence our colleagues to cooperate through example, logical argument and moral persuasion than by coercing through threats and warnings. The more coercive the means of influence, the less likely it is that the outcome will reflect the interests of both parties and the less legitimate it will be seen as by at least one of them.

▌ Value your colleagues. Feeling accepted, worthy and valued is a basic psychological need. We all want others to listen to our opinions and to accept our right to have views that differ from theirs. Accepting that need in others as well as in ourselves will increase the likelihood of working out differences and producing good outcomes.

Fisher and Brown make two other important points about establishing and maintaining good relationships. The first is to separate people from the problems. The severity of the differences between two individuals tends to affect the way they interact. If we want a relationship that can deal with differences we have to improve the process itself, independent of the substantive problems involved. Relationship issues concern the way we deal with people, such as clearly or ambiguously and honestly or deceptively. Substantive matters are, for instance, targets, deadlines, advice, contracts and terms and conditions. It seems best to work on the relationship–how we deal with each other–independently of substantive differences. Once we have a good working relationship it is then much easier to handle differences about substantive matters.

The second additional point about maintaining good relationships is to be unconditionally constructive. This means that we should do those things, and only those things, that are good for both the relationship and ourselves whether or not the other person reciprocates. In personal relations if we adopt tactics of copying each other's poor conduct the relationship is likely to deteriorate. If I put a bad interpretation on your conduct and copy it and you then follow my lead then communication breaks down, misunderstanding increases and trust disappears. An example is when two people each wait for an apology from the other. As time passes each becomes more upset or angry with the other and more determined not to apologize first. A belated and maybe grudging apology may be unable to put to rest a problem that could have been cleared up quickly by an unconditional apology by one person in the first place.

HANDLE CRISES CONSTRUCTIVELY

However effective you are as a team leader there is no way of avoiding periodic crises such as the loss of a major client, a significant business downturn, the loss of a highly competent colleague to a competitive firm or unethical or inappropriate conduct on the part of a team member.

When facing any business crisis there are three useful tips to bear in mind. The first is to ascertain the facts, distinguish causes and effects and identify the implications. The second is to decide whether you can handle the crisis alone or if you should involve other team members or colleagues elsewhere in the firm. The third is to pay particular attention to getting the communications right.

Let us look at these in a little more detail. The first step in crisis management is to identify the facts and separate these from rumours and conjecture. A particularly important task is assessing the implications of the crisis. If your team loses a major client, for example, there may be several consequences beyond the loss of fee income. Morale of colleagues could be badly affected. Other clients may hear about the loss and they may lose confidence in your team and take their business elsewhere. One of the hardest but necessary jobs is to face up honestly to the root cause of the problem. Maybe the loss of a long-standing valued client is due to complacency. Perhaps the team has taken the client for granted. Maybe you have neglected to nurture the client and provide first-class service in some way.

The second step is to decide whether you should handle the crisis personally or involve other colleagues inside or outside the team. If one of your team members has been accused of sexual harassment, for instance, you will probably wish to involve a human resources professional. The threatened defection of a major client might be avoided by a visit from the senior or managing partner. Occasionally, team leaders make the mistake of keeping a crisis to themselves because they fear that their reputations might suffer if information leaks out. More often than not the problem becomes generally known sooner or later and in the meantime they have lost the opportunity of involving others who can provide help.

The third step is to get the communications right. It is much more sensible to be open with your team members about the facts of a crisis and the way that it is being handled rather than trying to hide the details. Generally speaking, people are very quick to detect that something is seriously wrong even when they are not told about it. The problem with team members picking up and discussing scraps of information is that the issue becomes distorted and is surrounded with rumours and conjecture. It is crucial for you to be available during a crisis so that your team members can express their concerns, offer their views and seek your advice or reassurance. Being accessible is always important for team leaders but is especially so when things are going wrong.

Here are a few more tips for handling specific crises:

▌ If you lose a valued client tell all of your team members what is both known and not known about the reasons for losing the client at the earliest opportunity. Have a team discussion to analyse what went wrong. Explore how to avoid a similar loss in the future. Hold a brainstorming session to generate ideas for improving service quality to all other clients. Lift morale by reminding the team of its strengths. Share responsibility with your team members for the loss of the client and avoid allocating blame.

▌ If there is a significant business downturn that results in redundancies then tell the remaining team members the facts and help them to face up to the realities of the situation. Have brainstorming sessions with your colleagues to produce ideas for generating more business during the difficult times. Get everyone to contribute his or her thinking. This will have two benefits. You are almost certain to get some good ideas, and morale will be lifted among team members because everyone will be taking some positive actions. As things improve, acknowledge the assistance that everyone has given to helping the team through the crisis.

▌ If a highly valued colleague decides to leave and join a competitor then have a chat with the person concerned. If the reason for leaving is for career advancement or for a more lucrative income then agree how clients and colleagues should be informed and what they should be told. Maintain a good relationship and wish your colleague well for the future. Parting on amicable terms is important. Your ex-colleague will almost certainly talk about you and your firm to his or her new colleagues and clients. If the reason for leaving is a feeling of being undervalued it may be possible to provide reassurance and you might be able to effect a change of mind. Be careful, however, not to promise special treatment. Team colleagues may regard this as inequitable. That could produce a significant deterioration in morale and performance in the rest of the team.

▌ If one of your team members seriously breaches the code of ethics of the profession or of the firm or behaves unlawfully then the required course of action is usually evident from disciplinary rules and regulations. Because it is an unpleasant task, some team leaders procrastinate. It is crucial, however, to take the designated action immediately. Everyone needs to know what sort of behaviour is unacceptable, what the penalties are and that action will be taken if there is a serious breach of codes or rules. If the offence is so serious that the person concerned has to leave the firm then the facts should be communicated to team colleagues to avoid rumours and conjecture.

▌ Occasionally team members make significant mistakes that do not warrant disciplinary action. They may be errors of judgement or forgetfulness. It is helpful for team leaders to let everyone know that if that happens the best policy is to own up and learn rather than cover up. Most of us are willing to forgive if people are genuinely sorry and are willing to learn.

10

Results: Assessing team and individual performance

> *However beautiful the strategy,*
> *you should occasionally look at the results.*
>
> — (Sir Winston Churchill)

> *The more you understand what is wrong with a figure*
> *the more valuable that figure becomes.*
>
> — Lord Kelvin

There are two measurement traps for professional service teams. The first is to measure solely the financial results. Some people say these are the only ones that matter. Others say these are the only ones that you can measure accurately. The trouble with measuring just the financial results is that people are likely to concentrate on earning fees to the exclusion of everything else. It becomes all too easy to ignore long-term investment activities such as cultivating potential clients or raising the firm's profile by writing articles and running seminars. There is also the danger of neglecting personal skill development. Emphasis on current financial performance without also assessing and reacting to client perceptions of service quality may provide excellent results in the short term but could store up trouble for the longer term.

The second, and opposite, trap is to attempt to measure everything in detail and to inflict long lists of targets and performance standards on the people who are trying to get on with the job. I have even come across 'targets for setting targets' in some organizations! The effect is a demoralizing and time-wasting bureaucracy of form filling and red tape and an erosion of professional judgement. It is possible to develop a few relatively simple performance indicators and tools for teams and individuals that permit the assessment of the main variables in professional service work. These are financial health, success in the marketplace, service quality and personnel development. Good leaders will ensure that these measures are aligned with the objectives and strategy of the firm as a whole. At PricewaterhouseCoopers, teams assess how well they are doing against a balanced scorecard of key performance indicators. These are shown in Table 10.1.

In many professional service firms the management board or the partnership as a whole decides the performance indicators to be used throughout the firm. This is especially true of the financial standards. If this is the case in your firm and if you feel that the measures are not sufficiently comprehensive then why not discuss with your team the possibility of including one or two more? On the other hand if you feel that some of the firm's indicators are inappropriate for your team, or that there are too many of them, then why not make the point to the managing part-

Table 10.1   The balanced scorecard of key performance indicators at PricewaterhouseCoopers

People	Clients
Creating a common sense of purpose.	Building strong relationships with key clients.
Attracting, advancing and / or recognizing our diverse people.	PwC brand leverage and promoting a public profile.
	Creating more business opportunities.

Firm	Profits
Supporting and developing the global organization.	Income performance.
Transforming our support services.	Cash collections.
Knowledge sharing.	
Risk management and quality.	

ner? It is important to keep the criteria under review and to ensure that they are relevant and make a useful contribution to the effectiveness of your team and to the business generally. You want your team to keep its eye on the ball. The wrong measures can too easily divert energies away from the central issues. Effective leaders get agreement on how performance should be measured both with their own team members and with the firm's senior management.

MEASURE FINANCIAL RESULTS

Most professional service firms are partnerships and they either charge by the hour or on a fixed-fee basis for a specific service. There is a well-known formula governing profitability when hourly rates are used. This formula can be applied to a team as well as to the firm as a whole. It is:

Average equity partner profit = gearing × utilization × charge-out rates × margin × recovery

- *Gearing* (or leverage) is the ratio of junior to senior professional staff. (The use of the term 'gearing' here is different from the way that it is used in financial accounting. There it refers to the ratio of borrowings to shareholders' capital employed.) If a team can deliver its services with less senior time and more junior time it enhances profitability by getting more work done by people who cost less. Innovating in new processes, harnessing the benefits of electronic technology and investing significantly in improving skills are essential accompaniments. It is a very good way to drive up profits.

- *Utilization* is the number of hours charged. If utilization is increased, on average, within the team, then more profit can result. However, this has to be done with care. It is unwise, from a long-run perspective, for partners and other seniors to increase the number of their chargeable hours at the expense of time for leadership and obtaining new business. There is also a risk, from a profitability viewpoint, to expect trainees to charge a very high number of hours because the supervision costs will be so much greater.

- *Charge-out rates* are the fees charged per hour. If these can be increased through better service, innovations and a reputation for outstanding work then profitability can be enhanced significantly.

▌ *Margin* is the ratio of profit to fees. This is primarily influenced by productivity (utilization × charge-out rates) and gearing. The remaining costs of delivery are overheads. There may be room for some savings here but they are unlikely to be significant.

▌ *Recovery* is the proportion of work in progress that is billed. It is not unusual for people to under-bill. They feel that the level of work in progress is too expensive and that the client will object and perhaps go elsewhere next time. Increasing recovery by a very small percentage can produce a significant increase in profitability. The extra portion goes straight to the bottom line.

Teams in some firms have fee growth targets but no profit targets. Whilst growth of fees can be viewed as a measure of success in terms of position in the marketplace and the provision of career opportunities, it may be a delusion as far as profitability is concerned. Growth in fees, without a reduction in delivery costs or an increase in fee rates, will, broadly speaking, have a neutral effect on profitability. Measurement tools have a significant effect on people's behaviour. When teams and individuals have fee growth targets, but no profit targets, people are enticed to chase fees even if the work involved is unprofitable. The result is often high income and low profits for the team. It makes sense to have both profit and fee growth goals. Since in most medium to large professional service firms the nature of work undertaken varies considerably from team to team it is helpful for each leader and team to work out the most appropriate mixture of gearing, utilization and charge-out rates necessary to achieve their own profit-per-partner targets.

These days quite a few firms offer at least some of their services on a fixed-fee basis. They have learnt how to cost their service delivery, achieve a market-determined fee and generate a profit. In those firms that have been more used to charging by the hour, increased specialization and client pressures are now also leading to the use of fixed-fee contracts. A fee is quoted in advance for the service to be offered. Some professionals who are not used to the process find this a frightening prospect because it involves turning the conventional approach to costing on its head. The new requirement is to start with a market price and then work out how to deliver the service in a cost-effective and profitable manner. However, there are benefits. It becomes possible to build premiums into fees to cover investments in research, information technology, new methodologies and so on that may have been made previously. The problem of recovery (the proportion of work in progress that is billed) disappears. However, if your team provides fixed-fee services it is still important to calculate productivity (utilization × hourly rates) and gearing to determine the costs of service delivery.

There are two other useful financial measures. These are targets for unbilled work in progress and for receivables. They allow you to monitor the promptness both of billing and of clients paying. Both are important for cash flow and can impact on profitability.

The financial measures described here are mainly appropriate for partnerships. Some of the concepts, however, may be helpful to incorporated professional service firms and also to departments of professionals within corporations if they charge internally for their services.

JUDGE MARKET PERFORMANCE

One way to do this simply and economically is to have periodic team discussions on questions such as these:

- What proportion of our highly valued clients, that is those generating above a specified fee level, are we retaining from one year to the next?

- What proportion of our fees comes from new services offered within the last three years?

- What proportion of this year's fees is from new clients?

- What proportion of assignments that are pursued this year in competition with other providers have we won?

- What proportion of this year's fees has come from working in new industry, client or geographical sectors?

- What proportion of this year's new clients has fallen into our highly valued client category?

You and your team may find it helpful to formulate annual targets for some of these questions and then to monitor how well you are doing.

ASSESS SERVICE QUALITY

Some professionals still make the mistake of assuming that high-quality technical work means high-quality service. Of course the quality of work is critically important but the provider of professional services is probably judged more often on manner and style. Buyers of professional services usually ask themselves 'Do I like and do I trust this provider?' Positive answers to these questions usually result if the professional is a good listener, keeps to promises about deadlines, keeps the client informed about progress and is easily accessible when needed. It is important therefore for the team members to check out their competence through such mechanisms as assignment debriefings, informal discussions with clients, the use of feedback questionnaires and postings on electronic Web-based noticeboards. It is helpful for teams to store this information and then decide what needs to be done. For instance, what action is necessary immediately to respond to, and deal with, a client's concern? What changes need to be made to bring about improvements in service for the longer run?

Here are some examples of the issues that need to be considered to get good feedback on service quality:

▌ Was the assignment tackled thoroughly?

▌ Were problems diagnosed well?

▌ Were the solutions creative?

▌ Were promises on deadlines kept?

▌ Did we listen carefully to what the client had to say?

▌ Were our communications free of jargon?

▌ Did we let the client know in advance what we intended?

▌ Was the client kept informed about progress?

▌ Were we available when needed?

▌ Did we give comprehensive explanations for what we had done?

▌ Did we take the initiative in communicating with the client?

▌ Were we thoroughly informed about the client's business?

▌ Did we make the client feel important?

This is not an exhaustive list of service quality questions. You will think of others that are particularly relevant to the nature of your work and clients.

The business advisory services firm PricewaterhouseCoopers invites clients to complete feedback forms at the end of each engagement. The essence of the document is shown in the box 'PricewaterhouseCoopers:

Your response helps our response', and John Martin, Director – Clients and Markets, has this to say about the benefits:

> Quality of service is a key driver in our business and dialogue with our clients is a critical element in ensuring that we understand their needs and the expectations we aim to meet or surpass. Feedback indicates that we achieve this objective in over 95% of client engagements. We are proud of this success, but not complacent. We need to ensure that the trend continues to be upward and that we keep a sharp focus on the quality of our planning with key individuals at our clients to set the right objectives for each specific engagement.
>
> One of the pleasant surprises as we developed our feedback mechanism was the openness, which we found in client feedback. We set up the survey process to be independent and gave clients the option not to share feedback with the engagement team. We thought that this might be a common request but in practice found that confidentiality has rarely been used to give anonymous criticism. In fact, a recent review of feedback seems to indicate that 'sparing the blushes' is a more common motivation for not sharing feedback with the team.

PRICEWATERHOUSECOOPERS: YOUR RESPONSE HELPS OUR RESPONSE

We would like your feedback on how PwC performed on our recent engagement. Please indicate:

'Importance to you' and 'Your satisfaction with' from 10 (=high) to 1 (= low)

1. Meeting your needs and expectations – how satisfied are you that the PwC team:
   agreed detailed requirements with you?
   performed in line with the agreed requirements?

2. How satisfied are you that:
   we had sufficient understanding of your business needs?
   we had sufficient understanding of your business sector?
   we provided high-quality service?
   we managed our international service to you? (where applicable)

Are there any areas where you would like the team to be more proactive in future?

3. Working with you – how satisfied are you that:
   we used clear and effective oral and written communication?
   we kept you sufficiently informed of progress?
   we were easy to contact?
   we were responsive and attentive to your requests?
   Please make any comments/suggestions.

4. Overall, did our people relate well with your people?

5. How did individuals on the PwC team perform? We welcome specific comments:

6. To what extent did we deliver value to your organization?

7. Please rate your level of overall satisfaction with PwC, on this assignment.

Please add any additional comments you believe would be helpful to us:

Completed by:
Position:
Date:

The PwC team would value your feedback: however, in exceptional circumstances, if you would rather it is not distributed to the team please tick:

Thank you for your feedback.

Please return in the envelope provided to:

EVALUATE YOUR INVESTMENT IN PEOPLE

Although there are one or two useful measures, such as staff turnover and retention rates, for the firm as a whole, they have little meaning if applied to relatively small teams. However, it is a good idea for you and your team members to review personal development goals and achievements. This is probably best done on an individual basis. There are some comments on this process later in the chapter.

Some firms use surveys to test people's satisfaction with jobs, relationships, development opportunities, communication and so on. They are useful indicators of morale. If problems are highlighted then the firm can take action. Leaders may also find it helpful to discuss the results with their teams and to decide if specific changes need to be made in the ways that they work. You can see the sort of questions that law firm DMH use in their surveys in the box 'DMH staff survey 2001'. The questionnaires are completed anonymously. Personnel and Administration Director Denzil Jones sums up the benefits:

> We decided to conduct our first staff survey in 1999 in the run-up to our application for Investors in People accreditation. We engaged the help of a consultant to help us design the survey and to analyse and present the results so that individual responses were treated in strictest confidence and we had an independent view of the results.
>
> At the time of the first survey, we were aware that we had still some way to go in fulfilling the Investors in People criteria and approached the exercise with some trepidation. Although the survey confirmed some of our views it also demonstrated that we were better than we thought we were in a number of areas, which gave managers a boost. However, it demonstrated that the question of 'fair' pay was a major issue and the management team set about addressing the problem.
>
> By the time of our second survey in 2001, we had achieved our Investors in People accreditation and the survey gave us heartening reassurance that we had improved in practically all areas (with over 95 per cent agreeing or strongly agreeing that DMH is a good place in which to work). We were also pleased to see that the pay question was being successfully addressed. One disappointing area was 'internal communications', which had not improved to the extent we thought they should have done. As a result, we asked our consultant to carry out an in-depth review of the issues. This included discussions with groups of staff. As a result we have been taking further action to strengthen such things as internal group meetings and induction training and have recently launched a DMH intranet.
>
> Staff surveys are now an integral part of our management process. They are essential tools. We use them to find out how well we are achieving our goals and to identify issues that need to be tackled. No matter how well you think you are doing there is nothing better than to ask other people for their opinion – you may be surprised.

DMH STAFF SURVEY 2001

Respondents were asked to indicate if they strongly agreed; agreed; disagreed; or strongly disagreed with the following statements:

- I have a good understanding of the broad aims and direction of DMH.
- Our group holds regular meetings to discuss how well we are doing.
- I have every opportunity to make suggestions to improve how things are done.
- I am kept regularly informed about the things I need to know.
- I understand how my job contributes to the success of my group.
- I am actively encouraged to develop my skills.
- I am aware of the training and development opportunities that are available and how to access them.
- I am provided with effective day-to-day support, coaching and on-the-job training.
- I am always clear when attending training what the objectives are and how it will help me in my work.
- Following training I have sufficient opportunity to discuss what I have learnt and how to use it.

Only those respondents who had joined within the previous six months were asked to answer the next two questions:

- When I first joined I was effectively introduced to my job and helped to understand the organization.
- I was given the training I needed to do my first job effectively.

- I have sufficient opportunities to discuss with my manager how I am performing.
- If I do well my efforts are appreciated.
- We work consistently well together in our group.
- I am given enough authority and responsibility to do my job effectively.
- We have real commitment to high levels of client service in our group.
- I have confidence in the leadership of DMH.
- My pay is fair for the job I do and the effort I put in.
- People within the firm always treat me with respect.
- DMH is committed to putting people first.

▌ On the whole DMH is a good place to work.

Only those who were not group heads, team leaders or managers were invited to answer the next question:

▌ Our group is led effectively.

Only those who were group heads, team leaders or managers were invited to answer the remaining questions:

▌ I am clear about what is expected of me as a manager.
▌ I feel that I have been given enough support and training for my role as manager.
▌ The development of our staff is clearly linked to the aims and objectives of DMH.
▌ I could give examples of how the training and development activities have improved the performance of my team and DMH.

Respondents were given the opportunity to indicate the most important thing that they would do if they were running the firm.

They were finally invited, by ticking the appropriate boxes, to indicate the department in which they worked and the broad category of job that they held.

HOLD CONSTRUCTIVE PERFORMANCE REVIEW AND CAREER DEVELOPMENT DISCUSSIONS

Most firms have 'performance management' or 'appraisal' systems. They often have a bad name. People complain that they feel like end-of-term school reports. Frustration is caused by endless form filling. They are often backward looking with little emphasis on career development. Appraisers sometimes complain that they feel like 'God sitting in judgement'. They are uncomfortable and treat the process as a chore to be got over with as quickly and as painlessly as possible. At worst the process becomes a bureaucratic, mechanical and 'Frankenstein' nightmare in which the original good intentions of helping people to improve their performance and their careers are almost forgotten in the pressure to complete endless forms and documents. Nevertheless, well-conducted one-to-one discussions with team members are valuable. They provide an opportunity to learn from past performance and to set goals for future work and career development. A record of conclusions and intentions is necessary, but extensive documentation is best avoided. If you work for a firm that requires the completion of large amounts of paperwork, and if people feel that this has dubious value, then why not make the case for its reduction?

When there is an organizational requirement for periodic performance review and career development discussions then there is sometimes a temptation for team leaders to neglect day-in-and-day-out informal coaching. They are not alternatives. Good leaders do both. Regular coaching, done well, helps people to capitalize on their strengths, live up to their potentiality and improve their day-to-day performance. The periodic formal discussions provide the opportunity to take a broader view and to review performance against previously agreed longer-term objectives. They are also useful for formulating new or revised objectives that are congruent with the purpose of the firm and the team and for agreeing personal development goals. They can also be used to discuss and agree desirable improvements in the use of skills. Here are some thoughts about handling the process constructively and sensitively:

▌ Assessing performance against objectives is not done to allocate blame or find scapegoats when things go wrong. It is to identify steps for improvement and agree plans for implementation. Effective team leaders help people to set their own challenging but achievable goals. They make sure that the objectives are written in such a way that results can be measured or assessed against them. They ensure that the objectives for individuals are congruent with those of the team and of the firm as a whole. Good leaders encourage people to evaluate their own performance and they help them if necessary to identify options for improvement.

It is helpful to keep the old management saw 'What gets measured gets done' in mind. There is a well-known story, possibly apocryphal but probably true, about a bus company. Complaints from passengers wishing to use the bus service that the drivers were speeding past queues of people with a smile and wave of the hand have been met by a statement pointing out that it is impossible for the drivers to keep to their timetable if they have to stop for the passengers. Far more seriously, in May 2003 it was alleged that a number of the most highly rated hospitals in Britain had the worst patient death rates. The rating system was based on key targets and indicators. But, apparently, none of the targets that hospitals had to meet to get star ratings was clinical!

In a similar vein, if your team members have fee-earning objectives but no marketing objectives, don't be surprised if they neglect their marketing obligations. Obvious though this is, it is far from unusual to find objective setting confined to the more easily measured financial responsibilities. This happens just as much for individuals as it does for teams. It is probably a good idea to aim for one or two objectives for each major area of responsibility. Examples for professional people might include the amount and profitability of technical work; quality of service to clients; contributions to the marketing effort; contributions to helping others, for example coaching colleagues and supervising trainees; and contributions to firm-wide activities such as projects and presentations at conferences. Objectives for support people will vary and depend on the precise nature of their work. For team leaders themselves, objectives for the leadership aspects of their work are clearly desirable.

It is important for objectives to be accompanied by simple action plans, which indicate what needs to be done and by when. These make it easier to monitor progress. They also provide a check that the goals have realistic time-spans and that they are unambiguous.

▌ Personal development goals are concerned with the acquisition of new knowledge and skills to aid the realization of longer-term career aspirations. They are statements of what needs to be learnt, how and by when. The discussion is likely to include a consideration of learning preferences, organizational convenience and cost effectiveness. Are training courses appropriate or is planned experience through secondments a more attractive option? What part can reading and the use of interactive computer software play in the realization of the goals? Do arrangements need to be put in place for mentoring? Will research projects be helpful?

▌ When you meet with your colleague to review performance and talk about career development it is probably best to start by looking back at what has happened since the last discussion. Why not begin by inviting him or her to make an assessment of performance against the objectives set last time? If you both have the same perceptions then that is well and good. If your team member's assessment is tougher than yours then it is an easy and pleasant job for you to offer your evaluation. If on the other hand your assessment is that performance was not as good as your colleague believes then you will need to give feedback carefully and constructively in the way that was described in Chapter 7. Bear in mind one very important point. If the objectives in the first place were formulated with precision, and are unambiguous, then your assessment and that of your colleague are more likely to be aligned. When performance is not up to scratch you will need to agree on what needs to be done to bring about an improvement in the future. A good way to do this is to use the coaching style described in Chapter 7. Ask questions to raise awareness about the current and desired levels of performance. Explore the options available for making progress and from these seek a commitment from your colleague to specify actions that will result in an improvement.

The next step is to review progress made towards the personal development goals agreed last time. It is not uncommon for these to be neglected in the hurly-burly of the job. The task of the team leader here is to give lots of encouragement and to stress the importance of investing time and energy in becoming more distinctive and valuable. Nobody can rest on their laurels and have a worthwhile professional career these days. There is a huge responsibility for leaders to ensure that their people do more than pay lip service to personal development when the pressures of the day-to-day job often seem to be so overwhelming.

The last point of the discussion is usually devoted to revising objectives and setting new ones for the period ahead. The process usually works better when you invite your colleague to make the running. Once again the coaching style described in Chapter 7 can be used to great effect. Your questions can follow the pattern: how are you doing currently; what point do you want to reach and by when; what are the possible ways of getting there; and what will you actually do?

Performance review and career development discussions are useful. The trick is to keep them simple and to the point and to keep the paperwork to a minimum. Conduct discussions with sensitivity, focus on the future and use them primarily to give encouragement and help.

National law firm DLA's guidelines for its performance management system highlight the main points to take into account. They are:

▌ to assess performance against clear criteria;

▌ to identify opportunities for development so that individual potentiality can be realized;

- to identify objectives and establish an action plan to achieve them;

- to identify training needs, build on strengths, resolve areas for improvement and ensure progressive professional development;

- to facilitate a frank and open discussion;

- to ensure that development takes place within the context of the firm's overall business strategy.

The firm's guidance notes and training seminars stress that performance management is a process in which the objectives and actions of all participants should be kept under continual review. According to Human Resources Director Robert Halton, this is at the heart of the way that DLA does business:

> Our performance management process is the vehicle for delivering the firm's strategy – it allows plans to be divided into achievable objectives and lets people know how they contribute to the success of the firm.

Part Three

Bringing new people on board

11

Selection: Getting the right people into the jobs

It is as well, when judging a friend,
to remember that he is judging you with the same godlike
and superior impartiality.

— (Arnold Bennett)

Medium to large professional service firms generally have human resource staff who make the recruitment and selection arrangements, give general guidance on interviewing and testing techniques and advise on the stipulations of employment legislation. In addition they usually participate in the selection process and bring their expertise into play. However, team leaders are accountable for their teams' results and it is appropriate, therefore, that they have a major say in who is selected. It is certainly a good thing for them, at the very least, to be involved at the shortlist stage and thereafter. It is desirable for them, accordingly, to have the skills to conduct effective interviews, assess the results of selection tests and make reasonably objective judgements about people's attributes.

SELECT PRIMARILY FOR BASIC ABILITY, ATTITUDE AND CULTURAL FIT

Professional service firms with a good record for taking on able people usually place a higher value on basic ability and attitude of mind than on specific technical skills. When people are selected for traineeships, most of the technical skills are provided subsequently through training, coaching and mentoring. When qualified and experienced professionals are hired for more senior posts, then, of course, technical competence is important. Nevertheless if some of the skills are not in evidence then it is possible to help people to acquire them. What is difficult, on the other hand, is to change people who do not have the right attitudes and values and who are unlikely to fit in with the firm's culture. Professionals need to be very accomplished in dealing with clients and colleagues. They need to be almost obsessive about providing outstanding service. Ideally they should be good team players. They must have drive, initiative and organizing ability and the willingness to share and implement new ideas. Although these attributes can, to some extent, be developed they are to a large extent a function of people's attitudes and character.

Three professional service firms that take this lesson to heart are business advisers PricewaterhouseCoopers, law firm DLA and advertising agency Ogilvy & Mather. Ed Smith, UK Board Member at PricewaterhouseCoopers, says:

> We receive 20,000 applicants for 700 traineeships each year. Academic qualifications get people to the starting gate. We then sort people out on the basis of teamwork skills, use of initiative, confidence, willingness to take risks and evidence of some creativity and entrepreneurship. The latter quality is in relatively short supply among those attracted to the accountancy profession but extremely important to our sustainable growth.

Robert Halton, Human Resources Director at DLA, has this to say:

> When we recruit new people we pay a lot of attention at the selection stage to whether or not candidates will fit into our culture. For example, as far as trainees are concerned a good degree gets people to the door. We then run assessment exercises and have interviews to check out behavioural competencies that reflect our cultural values. For example, we test teamworking attributes such as empathy, the ability to work

well with other people and getting stuck into a joint effort. Another example is the extent to which they take initiatives. That tells us something about their drive to deliver good results. We also try to form a judgement about their potential ability to provide high-quality service to clients beyond technical competence. When we recruit qualified lawyers, of course, we pay attention to the candidates' technical experience but again we place great emphasis on whether or not they will work well in our culture. The same goes for support staff recruitment. Although our human resource people manage the recruitment and selection process, the leaders of law teams make the final selections. They are all trained in selection techniques. We are a people business, and selecting good staff is a vital part of the leadership process in our view.

Tim Solomon, Managing Partner at the London office of Ogilvy & Mather, comments:

As you would expect in an advertising agency we look for people at all levels who are enterprising and have creative flair. We need people who are good at dreaming something up. It all starts with the letters of application. Those that stand out and appeal to us are in some ways novel. They are not full of corny gimmicks but are genuinely original.

During the selection process we get further data by saying to candidates for instance 'You are going to open a new bar – tell us how it will be unique.' Candidates are given some time to think about it and then respond. Above all we don't want clones. Having said that, we don't want people who are likely to be dissonant with our basic values either. These beliefs have stood the test of time and go back to the founder of the business, David Ogilvy. Although we are now part of a large international group, WPP, we still live by those values within Ogilvy & Mather itself. Among the more important are putting brands first; enthusiasm for entrepreneurs and inventive mavericks; encouraging candour, curiosity, originality, intellectual rigour and civility; having high professional standards; treating each other with kindness; prizing confidence and discouraging arrogance (a fine line); respect for the intelligence of our consumer audiences; judging ourselves as being successful only when brands have become more valuable; and finally an abhorrence of toadies, prima donnas and office politicians. We try, during the selection process, to assess how well candidates will fit into our culture just as much as testing their analytical, creative, communications and relationship abilities.

SPECIFY THE CRITICAL ABILITIES AND ATTITUDES THAT THE SUCCESSFUL CANDIDATES MUST HAVE

The wrong people are sometimes hired because selectors fail to identify the few abilities and attitudes critical for success. When you have to fill a vacancy in your team, or if you are involved in selecting trainees, make sure that a specification of the attributes required is drawn up. Precision in defining qualities is important so that interviews and tests can be structured in ways that will result in relatively easy and objective assessments. You will probably want to choose some criteria that reflect the attributes of your more successful people. It will also be helpful to think about how your business environment is changing and specify some further criteria that reflect future rather than past needs.

The criteria that law firm DLA currently use for selecting trainee solicitors are shown in the box 'Criteria, definitions and sample questions used by DLA when selecting trainee solicitors'. The extent to which candidates meet the criteria is assessed at interviews undertaken by senior lawyers and human resource staff. In addition candidates are required to undertake some exercises that are used to test logical thinking, analysis of data and dealing with time pressures.

CRITERIA, DEFINITIONS AND SAMPLE QUESTIONS USED BY DLA WHEN SELECTING TRAINEE SOLICITORS

Communication skills

Ability to listen; reply perceptively; organize thoughts; think quickly; use language well; sound confident and reassuring; relaxed; polished.

Impact

Commands respect through professional manner; seems in control; outgoing; sociable; able to mix at all levels.

Adaptability

Settled into interview; would adapt to work environment; ability to change style in different situations.

Motivation

- Why law?
- Why commercial law?
- What do you enjoy about your legal studies?
- What action have you taken to find out about legal firms that interest you?
- How did you select the firms to apply to?
- Where do you want to be in 10 years' time?
- What motivates you?
- Tell me about your work experience placements.
- What do you think a career as a solicitor will offer you?

Team skills and leadership

- Have you ever had responsibility for organizing a group of people as a team?
- Are you a leader or a team player?
- Have you ever had a problem with any of your housemates and how did you deal with the situation?
- Have you ever had a difficult boss and how did you handle that person?
- Can you give me an example of when you have shown initiative?
- What would you do if, as a trainee solicitor, you discovered a mistake in your work and it had already been sent to the client?
- What positions of responsibility have you held?
- How would your friends describe you?

Planning and organization

- Are you an organized person?
- How do you manage your time?
- How do you strike a balance between study/work commitments and your leisure interests/sporting activities?
- Describe how you have planned and organized an event or project.
- Have you ever had to do more than one thing at the same time – how did you prioritize?

Analysis and judgement

- How will studying law be relevant to practising law?
- Describe the most complicated project or complex task you have ever had to organize – how did you tackle it and what did you do when you encountered problems?

- Describe a time when you made a major decision – how did this come about?
- What skills are needed to be a good solicitor?
- Summarize the role of a commercial lawyer in one sentence.
- Greatest strength, greatest area to be developed and greatest achievement to date.

Resilience and stability

- Describe a time when someone was critical of something you had done – how did you react?
- Tell me about the most difficult person you have ever had to deal with.
- Tell me about a time when you have been under great pressure at college/work.
- Did you encounter any problems during your year out – how did you solve these?

Commercial awareness

- What do you know about DLA?
- Why is a European association important to our clients?
- What are the threats to the legal profession?
- Do you think multidisciplinary practices should be allowed?
- Tell me about a newspaper story you are following.
- How would you market DLA to potential clients?

ACHIEVE A BALANCED TEAM THROUGH SELECTION

Dr Meredith Belbin has shown (1981), through his research, that all members of business teams have a dual role. The first is the functional one, which in professional service firms involves the use of technical, client relations, sales, marketing, administrative, management and leadership skills. The second role is what Meredith Belbin calls the team role. All of us who work in teams are aware of the fact that some people are good at coming up with bright ideas and others prefer to put ideas under the microscope and test them. We notice that some people are very anxious to get issues finalized and tasks allocated. Other team members are good at clarifying goals and promoting decision making. Some people are good at steering conversations and finding ways round obstacles and yet others can be relied upon to turn ideas into practical action in a disciplined fashion. Dr Belbin's research shows that it can be helpful to a team's efforts to have a number of different 'temperament types' of this sort to play off and balance each other. Indeed there is some evidence to show that teams comprising a mixture of temperaments produce better results than those consisting of people with teamworking characteristics that are similar to each other.

The implications for recruitment are clear. Selection of new people provides the opportunity to reflect on the existing make-up of the team. If it would be beneficial to achieve a better balance of team roles, then people with temperaments that are not currently present can be sought. So, for instance, if the team has a number of participants with analytical strengths but is short of ideas people, the selection process can be used to identify candidates who not only have the required technical skills and the right values and attitudes but can also demonstrate a track record of creative thinking.

INTERVIEW EFFECTIVELY

When you have specified the qualities that you are looking for, you can decide which of them should be assessed through the interviewing process and which ones should be judged by other mechanisms such as tests. This is an important step in getting the best out of interviews. In addition success is more likely to occur if the following interviewing guidelines are borne in mind:

- Acknowledge that for many reasons of which you are unaware the behaviour of candidates at interviews may not be typical.

- Keep the importance of appearance in perspective and trust few popular notions.

- Be aware of your own prejudices and try not to let them influence your judgements.

- Be aware that when anxious or threatened a person's main concern is to protect self-esteem and only secondly to convey an accurate picture of reality.

▍ Behaviour reflects the way that people see things. Your prediction of behaviour in a situation will be more accurate the more you understand the other person's way of judging the world.

▍ Beware of the trap of artificially filling gaps in your knowledge about a candidate, after the interview, because of a desire to give a rounded impression of the person.

▍ Gather as much evidence as possible about behaviour before making judgements about personality.

▍ In order to see the real person you want a candidate to be as relaxed as possible. You won't see the real person if the candidate is stressed.

▍ You are trying to find out if the candidate has qualities that you are looking for. Don't try to impress by demonstrating your cleverness, experience, wit or power.

▍ Make notes of what is said after checking that the candidate doesn't mind.

▍ Use open questions: 'Tell me about . . . ' Try to minimize the use of closed questions that give rise to yes and no answers: 'Have you . . . ?' and 'Can you . . . ?' Use comparative questions: 'What did you find most difficult about . . . ?' Follow up with probe questions beginning with interrogatives: 'How . . . ?' 'When . . . ?' 'What . . . ?' 'Where . . . ?' Remember the value of the pause. The candidate should be talking much more than you.

▍ It is clearly inappropriate to have a scripted list of questions. Each interview is dynamic with the flow dependent upon the responses from the candidate. As long as you are clear about the information that you need to assess then appropriate questions can be formulated by listening carefully to the responses. In order to probe effectively it is helpful to sequence questions with care. Here are a few examples.

If you wish to assess risk-taking capabilities you could follow a sequence like this:
– What is the riskiest decision that you have taken?
– What made it risky?
– Was it right?
– How did you assess that?

If you wish to assess the ability to organize work and use time well you could follow a sequence like this:
- What type of reports have you had to write?
- How do you go about report writing?
- How do you find sufficient undisturbed time for concentration?

If you wish to assess the ability to provide high-quality service you could follow a sequence like this:
- Please give me two or three examples of good service that you have provided.
- How did you know that your client regarded those as examples of good service?
- What do you do if you find it difficult to deliver the service to which you are committed?

If you wish to assess the ability to influence others and make things happen you could follow a sequence like this:
- Please tell me about an occasion when you have had to sell ideas and influence others to take action.
- How did you convince your colleagues about the merit of your proposals?
- How did you ensure that action, once agreed, was carried out?
- How did you gain cooperation to turn the ideas into action?

USE SELECTION TESTS AS WELL AS INTERVIEWS

Some firms use psychometric tests, including reasoning, intelligence and personality profiling, as part of their selection processes. Generally speaking these are handled by trained specialists in the human resource function or by external consultants. The results and their significance are made available to other selectors, including the team leaders, for consideration along with the rest of the information about the candidates. Many firms take the view that the objective information about people that is made available from psychometric tests, when added to all of the other data about candidates, does improve predictions about future performance. When they are used it is clearly important for those team leaders involved in the selection process, as well as the human resource specialists, to be trained to interpret the results.

It is well worth while to design and use what are sometimes described as 'situational tests' as part of the selection arrangements. These provide opportunities for candidates to demonstrate their abilities, or potentiality to develop competence, in specific aspects of work. For example, if it is important that people have the skills to present information to groups of colleagues or clients then candidates can be asked to prepare and give short presentations on an agreed topic to the selectors. It is possible to assess teamworking abilities, including support for and cooperation with others and the ability to provide and assess ideas, by getting candidates to undertake a group exercise that is observed by the selectors. Requiring candidates to explain a technical issue to a layperson, and to check for understanding, is a good way to assess communication skills. Information contained in CVs and application forms and obtained from interviews, whilst very valuable, is usually insufficient to provide a reasonably objective assessment of the existing and potential capabilities of the candidates. Situational tests, used to assess some of the critical qualities that you are looking for, in addition to all of the other sources of information, provide an excellent way of giving a rounded picture of each of the short-listed applicants.

An effective selection process takes up a considerable amount of time. It is not cheap therefore. There are firms that mistakenly cut corners to save money. Getting effective people into jobs is important in all organizations. It is crucial in professional service firms where the most significant asset, by far, is the human one. A good selection process that involves interviews with human resource specialists and team leaders and that incorporates carefully designed situational tests reduces the risks considerably of hiring the wrong people. Firms that are serious about selection put applicants through more than one round of interviews and exercises. There are two benefits. The first is that it ensures that those who survive the process have been carefully scrutinized. Secondly, it promotes the feeling among those who are hired that the firm is really worth joining because it takes the recruitment process so seriously.

REMEMBER THAT SELECTION IS A TWO-WAY PROCESS

It is helpful for you keep in mind that just as you wish to get the facts about the candidates they want to know the truth about your firm and the team in which they are going to work. If you misrepresent the nature of the work and its challenges, or the firm's policies and culture, then this will become apparent very quickly to those who join you. Motivation, and therefore performance, will immediately take a knock. The selection process works best when the selectors are completely honest.

It is also important to remember that when you are involved in recruiting new people you are in effect seen by the applicants as an ambassador for your firm. Treating candidates in a dignified manner, and in particular ensuring that those who fail to make the grade receive thanks for their interest and a clear explanation for their rejection, is imperative. People who are treated in a cavalier fashion may have some very harsh things to say to others about the firm concerned.

ASSESS THE RESULTS
OF THE SELECTION PROCESS

Human resource specialists who know their stuff attempt to validate selection methods against the performance of the people selected so that the process can be modified and improved as time goes on. Some firms keep records of who interviews applicants. When recruits subsequently do especially well or poorly in their jobs the human resource people try to analyse what the interviewers saw or missed. As a result recruitment and selection can be made more effective. It is a good thing for team leaders to cooperate with this activity or press for it to occur if it does not already happen. Everything that can be done to improve the quality of the people who are taken on is very much in the firm's and the team's interests. It is a prime concern for team leaders.

12

Early days: Helping new people to fit in and nurturing trainees

*It is our responsibilities, not ourselves,
that we should take seriously.*

— (Peter Ustinov)

Most firms these days have some sort of induction programme for their new people. Typically, newcomers are given information about the firm's goals, policies, culture, markets, clients and reward systems. Invariably presentations are supported with written information and access to Web sites. Despite this, it is very easy for people who have recently joined the firm to feel that they are being left to sink or swim unless team leaders take great care to reinforce and extend whatever formal induction processes exist. The chances are that if this is not done well then staff turnover will be greater than otherwise. Robert Halton, Human Resources Director at DLA, is very clear about the importance of induction and the critical role of team leaders in the process:

> A few years ago we surveyed people who had left the firm over an 18-month period. We found that the main reasons for people resigning were because they had not been led properly and

to get broader experience. These conclusions flew in the face of the conventional wisdom of the time that people left primarily to get more money. Our practice had been to recruit good people and let them get on with it. It was very much a sink-or-swim approach and it wasn't very good. Our partners were shocked and we set about establishing much better formal induction processes and clarifying the roles of team leaders, including their responsibilities for helping newcomers to fit in. In three years, annual turnover was reduced from 32 per cent to 16 per cent. We now take the induction process very seriously. The trick is to keep newcomers as well motivated as they were the day before they joined us. So we have formal induction programmes and it is the team leader's job to ensure that all of their new people attend. We also have a 'buddy' system. Each new recruit is allocated to a 'buddy' in the team who deals with any worries, questions and so forth and helps the newcomer to fit in. They have some lunches and drinks together to help the process along. It is the job of the team leader to ensure that the 'buddy' system works properly. Probably the most important role of the team leader in helping people to settle in is to give the right amount and right sort of work to move newcomers up the learning curve as quickly as possible. This means help and guidance, in other words good coaching.

INVEST TIME AND ENERGY TO HELP NEW PEOPLE TO SUCCEED

Here are a few tips for integrating new people:

▪ Make sure that new people receive the firm's formal induction programme as soon as possible. If for any reason they have to wait for a while before the next one is available, take them through the main points yourself and ensure that they have all of the relevant documentation.

▪ Introduce newcomers, personally, to each member of your team and to others in the firm with whom they are likely to be in contact during the first few weeks.

▪ Circulate e-mails to all of your team colleagues and to others, welcoming the new recruits and giving some information about where they come from and what they are going to do.

▌ Ask one of your support people to give some training on the electronic information and telecommunications systems to newcomers within a day of joining. You could also ask them to take newcomers on a tour of the office and to answer the many questions about administrative procedures that are likely to crop up.

▌ Hold a team meeting within two or three days of new people arriving to discuss assignments and clients and how the newcomers can contribute to the team's work.

▌ Involve new people in work as early as possible and personally introduce them to relevant clients. Give them a chance to accomplish something early on thus helping them to develop their own confidence and to give your colleagues confidence in them.

▌ Take the opportunity to have lunch with new recruits within two or three weeks of their arrival. Ask them for their first impressions and if there is anything more that you can do to help them become established members of your team.

▌ Invest some time to help new people with their work problems, to seek feedback and to integrate them into your team. Meet with them at, say, fortnightly intervals for the first six months.

▌ Give newcomers an opportunity to get to know team colleagues and other important contacts within the firm on a personal as well as professional basis. Set up some social events, lunches, dinners or trips to pubs to bring this about.

▌ Allocate assignments of a progressively more challenging nature during the first six months to help them to build their self-confidence and to demonstrate that they are making significant contributions.

The team leaders at the CBI put many of these ideas into effect when integrating new policy analysts and advisers into the organization. Deputy Director-General John Cridland puts it this way:

> In one sense motivation for us is easy. The CBI is a fun place in which to work. Young people in their 20s are at the centre of things with the opportunity to meet business leaders, senior politicians, civil servants and ministers. We have a high turnover of graduates, roughly 25 per cent per year, because

many of our people receive good job offers from our members. We understand this and accept it. So we have to get our new people up to speed very quickly to get the best out of them in the two or three or perhaps four years that they are with us. First-class induction is a must. Our personnel people provide a thorough formal induction programme. Our team leaders and their senior policy adviser colleagues then do plenty of coaching and mentoring. It is a sort of apprenticeship system with the need to ratchet up skills rapidly. In the second month our new policy advisers attend outside meetings with senior colleagues. Within six months they are leading for the CBI at meetings with senior civil servants on government committees or senior business members of the CBI. They do interviews on local radio after a few months. They make presentations to the regional CBI councils. They will be exposed to contacts in the European Union and so on. Our team leaders have to make sure, through their own efforts and those of their senior colleagues, that the young graduates quickly develop and use writing, presentation, media and meetings skills. In this way our people become integrated into our culture very rapidly. That helps to reinforce the motivation that comes, anyway, from being at the centre of things and having the opportunity to rub shoulders with interesting and influential people.

FORMAL INDUCTION AT THE CBI

As well as the work undertaken by the team leaders, the CBI provides a number of formal induction activities for its newcomers. On the very first morning they talk with a representative of the personnel department at which such matters as terms and conditions, policies and procedures and training are discussed. Then they have a meeting with their immediate team leaders at which their roles are reviewed in some detail and objectives are agreed for the first three to six months. The work of the directorates, CBI regional offices and the Brussels and Washington offices is explained. The immediate team leaders, at this stage, then take the opportunity to introduce newcomers to their directors, team colleagues, staff council representatives and other useful contacts. The third phase of the process is an induction day organized by the personnel department to give participants a broad view of the CBI's work. The history and structure are explained; the vision, mission and current aims and objectives are outlined; and the roles of all of the CBI directorates are elaborated.

Newcomers also have the opportunity, at this stage, to chat to the Director-General or Deputy Director-General. Plenty of time is given for questions.

Everyone also receives an induction pack, which includes important information about the CBI. Individuals can also use it to keep a record of their training and development and performance appraisals. It includes a welcome letter from the Director-General and details of the CBI's strategy, work plans, achievements and latest annual report and accounts. There are details of the CBI's training and development policy and its implications for newcomers. It provides comprehensive details on terms and conditions, health and safety and the organization's structure. There is a staff directorate and office plan.

The combination of this comprehensive induction programme organized by the CBI's personnel department and the coaching and mentoring work undertaken by team leaders and their colleagues ensures that new staff at the CBI are well integrated and brought up to speed rapidly.

NURTURE YOUR TRAINEES

If trainees are to stay well motivated and enthusiastic about working for your firm they need to develop their skills and knowledge quickly and effectively. There are two processes that are central to this need. The first is the way the people are assigned to their tasks and the second is the quality of supervision that they receive. It is the team leader's job to see that both of these are working well and that they satisfy the needs of the team, the firm and the individual trainees concerned.

A good scheduling system requires an appropriate balance between profitability, client service and skill-building considerations. It is clearly necessary to keep everyone busy, as otherwise profitability will suffer. It is also important to try to match staff with clients' needs. This will often go beyond the deployment of people with the technical skills that are needed by particular clients to matching the 'personal chemistry' of individual professionals with the client firms' representatives. Good assignment decisions often influence the possibility of follow-up business. However, the needs of professional development must also be met and not least those of trainees, who, by definition, need to learn as rapidly as possible. The assignment process is a major determinant of both the amount and the nature of skill development. The mixture of assignments, at an early stage in a professional's career, will determine how far that individual will become a functional expert, a sector expert or a generalist. As far as skill development is concerned it is also helpful for trainees to be assigned to a variety of senior people with different talents and styles. They are likely as a result to have far richer experiences and to learn more through undertaking a wider range of tasks in different ways. They will have the opportunity, also, to observe different approaches to interviews, negotiations, meetings and so on.

So that a good balance can be struck between keeping people busy, providing a good personal match between professionals and clients and providing skill development it is a good idea for the team as a whole to meet regularly to allocate trainees to assignments. It need not take too long. It is a good way of ensuring that all angles are covered. It also fosters collective responsibility among team members for ensuring that the three objectives of the scheduling process are achieved.

In some firms the quality of supervision of trainees is a hit-and-miss affair. This is for two reasons. Sometimes supervisors are not trained to do the job. Some may be good because they have an appropriate personal style and they may have learnt the arts from having been supervised well themselves, when trainees, by people who were talented leaders. Others may be found wanting. The second reason is that agreed guidelines for supervising trainees do not exist. Good team leaders ensure that those responsible for supervising trainees receive some training or coaching in the skills involved. They also engage their team colleagues in defining appropriate guidelines that everyone concerned commits to putting into effect. Teams will want to choose their own guidelines, but here are some possibilities to help you to think along the right lines:

▪ Trainees are told how their particular tasks fit into the objectives for the assignment.

▪ Supervisors receive effective coaching to help them to improve their performance (see Chapter 7 for the skills involved).

▪ Supervisors provide regular and prompt feedback on performance (see Chapters 6 and 7 for the skills involved).

▪ Supervisors are available without long delays when questions need to be asked.

▌ Trainees are encouraged to make their own decisions about their tasks.

▌ Trainees are encouraged to offer their thoughts on improving the ways that assignments are undertaken.

▌ Objectives, target dates, standards of performance and so on are agreed with trainees rather than imposed.

▌ Trainees are exposed progressively to more interesting and challenging work.

▌ Discussions are held regularly between supervisors and trainees on progress, perceptions, anxieties, career aspirations and job satisfaction.

▌ Supervisors encourage trainees to participate fully in team discussions.

▌ Supervisors provide help with skill development, outside the assignments themselves, by seeking out appropriate training programmes and reading material and providing opportunities for trainees to meet and talk with senior colleagues or useful people outside the firm.

▌ Supervisors give trainees the opportunity to accompany them at interviews, negotiations, meetings and so on and to discuss processes and outcomes afterwards.

▌ Supervisors let colleagues know about particularly effective pieces of work undertaken by trainees.

▌ Supervisors give trainees the opportunity to redo work that is not up to expectations, after discussions about what needs to be changed. Supervisors do not redo the work themselves.

▌ Supervisors show at least as much care and concern for trainees as for the assignments.

▌ Supervisors use delegation as a way of helping trainees to learn.

▌ Supervisors don't second-guess trainees; they ask them to explain.

▌ When trainees come to supervisors with problems about their work, the supervisors ask the trainees how they propose to handle them.

Many of these guidelines will appear obvious to those supervisors of trainees to whom the activity comes naturally. For others, they will, if followed, enhance supervisory performance. Good team leaders who chat informally with all members of their teams, including the trainees, will quickly discover if the supervisory guidelines are being followed. If they are not, it is the job of the team leaders to remind colleagues that the guidelines are in place and have been agreed by everyone. As time goes on, and if people are reminded about the importance of the supervisory guidelines, they become embedded in the culture. When that happens most professionals do their best to observe them.

There is a systematic and effective process for supervising trainees at DLA. Human Resources Director Robert Halton has this to say:

> We use associates (usually lawyers with a minimum of five or six years' experience) who have excellent technical skills to supervise trainees. This we believe is good news for the trainees and good news for the associates who develop their leadership skills in preparation for partnership. We teach associates how to supervise. The main stages are first to give good briefings for assignments with explanations of purpose. The second is to be available to clarify, and the third stage involves monitoring and the provision of feedback. We encourage trainees to go with associates to meetings with clients and colleagues to observe and learn.
>
> We are very keen on the idea that if things go wrong then trainees should not be torn off a strip. We want them to own up to problems early. The aim is to help them to learn from mistakes so that they don't happen again. We encourage them, if in doubt, to check and we tell them that there is no such thing as a stupid question as long as they don't ask it more than once. I think that it is an important part of a team leader's job to see that the associates undertake this supervisory role in the way, the right way, that I have described.

Part Four

Projects

13

Leading project teams

Planning is an unnatural process; it is much more fun to do something. The nicest thing about not planning is that failure comes as a complete surprise, rather than being preceded by a period of worry and depression.

— (Sir John Harvey-Jones)

When firms want to innovate or make changes they often set up a project team to produce recommendations. Examples include the development of a new service; the introduction of a new information technology system; modifications to the remuneration arrangements; fresh ways of seeking feedback from clients; a new staff development policy; changes to the performance review scheme; an office move; or an improved information database. Many professional assignments for clients may also be regarded as projects. The teams are usually made up of people from different departments who collectively bring a wide range of experience and expertise to the matter in hand. Although many of the attributes and tasks of an effective project team leader are the same as those required in leading a permanent team of professionals, there are also some important differences. This chapter is written to help those who find themselves, temporarily, in the role of project leader.

There are a few characteristics that are common to all projects. They have clearly defined objectives, success can be judged, they have definite timescales and they are unique although there may be similarities to other assignments. Because the individuals who comprise the team are usually drawn from different departments and have their regular day-to-day responsibilities to attend to, project leaders need considerable skill in holding the team together and delivering results. It is very easy for project team members, however well intentioned at the start, to neglect the project work in favour of undertaking their day-to-day professional tasks. The problem is sometimes compounded by the tacit or, in some cases, overt support for such behaviour from the regular professional service team leaders. Projects, because they are often concerned with innovation and change, are, by definition, important. A useful task for project team leaders at the outset is to get commitment from individual project team members to provide an agreed amount of regular time to the project. This commitment is likely to relate to time for individual contributions to the project as well as for attending project meetings. A wise project leader will also make it clear to the project sponsor and to the leaders of those professional service teams from which the project team members are drawn that he or she is only willing to lead the project if time commitments are given, honoured and supported by everyone concerned.

John Cridland, Deputy Director-General, describes the challenges for project leaders at the Confederation of British Industry:

> We have two sorts of projects. Some are concerned with changes to our work processes and others are set up to provide a multidisciplinary approach to policy work. One of our major difficulties is getting people trained in different disciplines to work together effectively. For example, we need some of our economists and some of our lawyers to work alongside each other on competition matters. The economists are there to provide a macro view. Because there are also micro legal issues at stake, then lawyers need to be involved as well. We do find quite often that, because of the very different training involved and the different assumptions that follow, there is a gap in communications and understanding. One way round the problem is to have generalists in the project team, and indeed the project leaders may well be generalists, to act as translators. They may help the team to develop an independent way of looking at issues. One way is through mind mapping or treating the problems in logical tree cause-and-effect terms. It is rather as though you have a

group of people, some of whom speak one language and others who speak another, and the only way that they communicate with each other is by speaking Esperanto. Another example is a project team concerned with the communication of intellectual property to members through the provision of electronically based summaries. Educationalists and environmental experts, for instance, may find it difficult to agree with media specialists on the ways summaries of information should be written. The generalists on the team can often provide the way through.

Our policy advisers work in dedicated professional teams for most of their time. This poses a problem when we want them to contribute to multidisciplinary project work. There are two difficulties. People tend to be tribal and given half a chance prefer to stay rooted in their regular teams. When there is a conflict of priorities the dedicated teams tend to win out. Another problem is the balance of power. There is a tendency for the leaders of dedicated teams to require that their work takes priority. It is rather like the England football team losing out to the clubs because the clubs will not cooperate sufficiently with release for training and the provision of rest time. The clubs have the greater power so they put their interests first.

We have some solutions. Sometimes, if the project is critical enough, we can allocate people to it on a full-time basis for a short period of time. This is easier with policy advice than with organizational change projects. Another way is for the dedicated team leaders to constitute a project team and to use their own team members to undertake work for the project on a sub-contracted basis. Most important of all, however, is to create a culture, which we are in the process of doing, where projects are seen as sufficiently important. We are now strengthening projects by giving them an appealing brand identity, a proper budget, including an analysis of the opportunity costs involved in working on projects rather than on regular activities, and by giving organizational backing to project sponsors and leaders to exercise more clout over the use of resources.

AGREE OBJECTIVES
AND PERFORMANCE CRITERIA

Generally speaking the sponsor (usually a senior member of the firm or maybe the partnership board as a whole) will indicate the broad scope of the project to be undertaken. A good way to get the project off to an enthusiastic start is for the project leader, with the team, to prepare a clear objective and performance criteria that can then be agreed with the sponsor. I believe that it is important for the team to make a major contribution to defining goals and standards by which the project can be assessed rather than simply to accept a directive from the sponsor. Better motivation, and therefore results, is likely to occur if team members, the project team leader and the sponsor are all in full agreement on these matters.

Objective

The project objective is a statement of the purpose of the project. Here is an example:

> To formulate a new pay policy that rewards corporate, team and individual performance and is capable of attracting and retaining first-class people.

Performance criteria

Performance criteria for most professional service projects cover quality, cost and time. Here are examples of quality criteria for the pay policy project:

> The partnership board and full partners' meeting accept the recommendations without the need for modification.
> Attitude surveys, among the staff, produce an average of 4 out of 5 or better on rating scales used for assessing the enthusiasm for the proposals.

As far as cost is concerned the project will be rated a success if the budget for expenses, supplies and project team members' time has not been exceeded. (It is a useful, but rare, discipline to budget for the opportunity cost, that is the time normally devoted to professional work that has to be given up for project tasks and meetings.) An element in the cost budget for the time to be given to project activities also helps to reinforce the commitment for such work that is so necessary but frequently difficult to secure.

As far as time is concerned the project will be considered a success if the outcomes are delivered by the target date for completion. For relatively large and complicated projects, meeting milestones that mark the end of particular phases will also be an indication of progress.

CREATE OPTIONS
BEFORE DECIDING WHAT TO DO

Usually there are several possible ways of achieving project objectives. Before deciding on a basic course of action it is helpful for you and the project team to brainstorm options and then to assess the pros and cons of each. The techniques described in Chapter 8 on teamwork may be used. It is very easy for a project team anxious to get on with the job to fall into the trap of 'groupthink' (also examined in detail in Chapter 8) at the outset. On a number of occasions I have seen project teams undertake quite a lot of work and then realize that they are on the wrong track. Usually this occurs when the team makes an early decision to pursue an approach that seems to be attractive but for which the analysis is superficial. As with so many things in life, too short a period of time devoted to thinking often results in time wasted in the action phase. Reworking parts of the project or even starting again becomes commonplace.

PLAN WITH PERSPECTIVE

When your team has decided on a basic course of action the next stage is to agree priorities, sequence and timing of steps. A good way to do this is to use perspective. This concept was popularized by Eddie Obeng in his book *All Change: The project leader's secret handbook* (1994). Get your team to assume that the project has been completed and then to imagine the tasks that would have been undertaken to get there. It is helpful to display the team's collective thinking visually, perhaps by writing the steps on post-it notes and sticking them on a whiteboard. In this way the information can be moved around to reflect developments in thinking. Figure 13.1 provides a simple illustration of this process by using an example of a project team set up to recommend more effective methods for obtaining feedback on service quality from clients. It illustrates the 'imagined tasks' involved in working through one strand of the project.

When you have completed the process illustrated in Figure 13.1 you can use it as a basis for allocating tasks to individuals. The post-it notes can be transferred to a chart with time along the horizontal axis and the names of team members on the vertical axis. It is helpful to have an individual owner, preferably a volunteer, for each task and to establish starting and finishing times. It is useful to insert time buffers if people believe that they have a very heavy workload. Time buffers are also valuable

Step 1   Define the project outcome, for example:

In order to have
developed more
effective ways of
seeking feedback
from clients

Step 2   Guess the major steps or sub-projects, for example:
we would have had to have . . .

found out which
methods of
feedback are
currently used by
the firm   and
determine if they
are good or bad

found out which
methods of
feedback are
effective in other
professional service
firms

reviewed the
literature and Web
sites on quality-of-
service client
feedback and
identified best
practice

generated and
evaluated ideas
for producing
novel ways of
seeking feedback

Step 3   Guess the tasks that need to be undertaken for each of the major
steps or sub-projects, for example:

In order to have
found out which
methods of
feedback are
effective in
other professional
service firms

we would have had to have . . .

selected 10
professional
service firms
from different
sectors

discussed client
feedback arran-
gements with
representatives
from the 10 firms
and collected
sample material

prepared a report
on the lessons
learnt about
effective client
feedback from
the 10 firms

Figure 13.1 Using perspective: the process of imagining a project has
been completed and the steps taken for getting there

whenever more than one activity must be completed before the next activities can be started. It is a good idea to make sure that project team members have tasks and times recorded in their diaries.

Although project planning computer software packages can be helpful, those that are based on critical path analysis are not especially relevant to most projects undertaken in professional service firms. There are two reasons. As we have seen, professionals usually give part of their time only to project work. Teams are seldom 100 per cent dedicated. Because people's time is limited it is more important to schedule that resource first and the tasks subsequently. Critical path analysis can help you to establish the best order for tasks to be done by identifying dependency constraints. The trouble with it is that it assumes dedication to the project by those undertaking the tasks. The second reason is that most professional service firm innovation and client projects, as far as their planning requirements are concerned, are too straightforward to justify its use.

You will want all of your team members to attend project team meetings held for generating ideas, reviewing progress and so on. It is generally regarded as good practice to fix dates for all meetings at the beginning. It is much easier to ensure a good attendance this way. Agreeing the dates with your project team colleagues at the start is part of the planning process.

COORDINATE AND CHECK PROGRESS

Coordination and control in professional service firms are difficult. Your team members usually come from different departments and have their regular and pressing work commitments. The project is likely to involve a wide range of tasks undertaken by different people, sometimes in parallel and sometimes in sequence. There are a couple of useful tips to help the process along. The first is to think about how much attention you need to give to the tasks undertaken by your team colleagues. A simple way to do this is illustrated in Figure 13.2.

The second thing to do is to raise and maintain awareness about what might damage the success of the project. This can be done at project meetings and on a one-to-one basis with team members. Ask them to keep you informed about events outside the project that might pose risks for it. An example might be a sudden increase in the day-to-day professional workload as a result of a colleague being ill.

The progress reviews at meetings provide the opportunity for the project leader and team members to reflect and learn from what has happened so far in the project. Was it expected or unexpected? What are

	Delegate these and ask to be kept informed if difficulties arise; otherwise check progress at project review meetings.	Delegate these and check progress at review meetings.
Does the team member already have the expertise and/or experience to do the task? Y E S		
N O	Work closely with the person concerned and check progress frequently. Do some coaching if that will help.	Pay attention to these only if they are late and provide help, including coaching, if necessary.

YES   NO

Is this task critical to the success of the project?

Figure 13.2   Coordinating and checking progress

the implications for us? What actions do we need to take to modify or remedy the situation?

WORK WITH THE STAKEHOLDERS

Apart from with the team members, the project leader needs to build and maintain good relationships with others who have an interest in the process and in the outcome. They are often described as stakeholders. The project sponsor (that is the person who, or body that, commissions the project) is clearly an important stakeholder. The others include those who may be affected by the results or have interests in the outcome, and people who supply services to the project team on, say, a subcontracted basis. If you are going to do this part of your job well you will need to be an effective negotiator, manage expectations well and be especially competent at keeping everyone fully informed.

Agreeing objectives and performance criteria might involve a negotiation. Your sponsor and your team may want broadly the same outcome but may differ on the precise wording of the objectives and may wish to establish rather different performance criteria for ensuring the success of the project. There may be other people in the firm with an interest in the project who want to see the results biased in a particular direction that suits them and their immediate colleagues. You may have to use your negotiating skills to deliver an outcome that gives them some degree of satisfaction but does not detract from the broader aims that you, your team and your sponsor wish to achieve. There may also be some negotiations required if you obtain services from suppliers and subcontractors such as externally resourced research.

Whether a negotiation is about contracts or resources, a family matter or even international affairs, it is commonplace for each side to take a position, argue for it and perhaps eventually make concessions to reach a compromise. On the face of it this may sound like a reasonably satisfactory process. After all, a compromise suggests that both parties will get something by looking for trade-offs or splitting the difference. It may produce a moderately good result but it is unlikely to be an optimum settlement. The main problem with bargaining in this way is that people often tend to lock themselves into their respective positions. The more we seek to defend our positions the more committed we become to them. Our egos become involved and the negotiation takes on the characteristic of face saving. As more attention is devoted to positions, the underlying interests of the parties tend to be forgotten. Agreements become less likely or the result is a halfway measure that does not really satisfy either party. The process is sometimes bedevilled with deceits, stonewalling and walkouts. It is a battle of wills. At worst, if the negotiators are 'hard' bargainers who use pressure and intimidation then relationships may be strained or even permanently damaged. People may stop talking to each other.

Some people are aware of the danger of bargaining toughly over positions. They go to the opposite extreme of making early offers and concessions and yielding frequently to avoid confrontations. They hope that by building and maintaining a friendly relationship, then mutually satisfactory outcomes will follow. The danger for the 'soft' negotiator, of course, is losing out, especially when facing someone who is playing a 'hard' game.

At the Harvard Negotiating Project described by Roger Fisher and William Ury in their book *Getting to Yes: Negotiating agreement without giving in* (1982), a different approach is recommended. The method, called principled negotiation, comprises four elements. These are:

▌ *People.* Separate the people from the problem.

▌ *Interests.* Focus on interests not positions.

■ *Options.*   Generate a variety of possibilities before deciding what to do.

■ *Criteria.*   Insist that the result be based on objective standards.

People

Separating the people from the problem means trying to get away from the notion that the negotiators are adversaries involved in a personal face-to-face confrontation. Rather it requires the parties to think of themselves as partners in a rational side-by-side search for a fair agreement that satisfies the interests of both. There are two ways that you can try to achieve this. The first is to build and maintain good working relationships before you begin to negotiate. The second is to recommend the benefits of a joint problem-solving approach and to seek agreement on doing it this way before you negotiate about the substantive issues. It is a form of 'talks about talks'.

Interests

Focus on interests rather than positions. The real problem in a negotiation lies not in conflicting positions but rather in the differences between each party's needs, concerns, desires and fears. Interests motivate people and they are usually the silent underpinning of positions. A classic example of identifying the real interests that underpinned positions was the Egyptian–Israeli peace treaty formulated at Camp David in the United States in 1978. Members of the Harvard Negotiating Project team were advisers. Israel had occupied the Egyptian Sinai Peninsula since the Six Day War in 1967. When Egyptian and Israeli representatives sat down together in 1978 to negotiate a peace, their positions were incompatible. Israel insisted on keeping some of the Sinai. Egypt, on the other hand, insisted that every inch of the Sinai be returned to Egyptian sovereignty. Time and again, people drew maps showing possible boundary lines that would divide the Sinai between Egypt and Israel. Compromising in this way was wholly unacceptable to Egypt. To go back to the situation as it was in 1967 was equally unacceptable to Israel.

Looking to their interests instead of their positions made it possible to develop solutions. Israel's interest lay in security; they did not want Egyptian tanks poised on their border ready to roll across at any time. Egypt's interest lay in sovereignty: the Sinai had been part of Egypt since the time of the Pharaohs. Egypt had only recently regained full sovereignty after centuries of domination by the Greeks, Romans, Turks, French and British. It was not about to cede territory to another foreign conqueror. At Camp David, President Sadat of Egypt and Prime Minister Begin of Israel agreed a plan that would return the Sinai to complete Egyptian sovereignty and, by demilitarizing large areas, would assure Israel security. The Egyptian flag would fly everywhere but Egyptian tanks would be nowhere near Israel.

Reconciling interests works because when you examine opposite positions for the underlying motivating interests it is possible to invent options that meet the interests of both parties. It is also possible to discover compatible interests that may be disguised when the attention is placed primarily on positions. Take the example of a project leader negotiating a completion date with the sponsor. The project leader may argue that nine months is needed to complete the project. The sponsor may press for six months. A compromise of seven and a half months if they simply focus on positions would satisfy neither party properly. Examinations of the interests of both might reveal a sensible solution. For instance, it might become apparent that the sponsor's real interest is a quick completion to satisfy commitments previously given to senior colleagues or clients. The project leader's motivation might be a high-quality piece of work that, given existing resources, requires a longer period for completion. Once these facts are revealed it may be possible to find a mutually satisfying outcome involving, for instance, the subcontracting of some of the project work or the inclusion of one or two extra team members. In this way the six-month deadline could be achieved (the sponsor's interest) and a quality job could be guaranteed (the project leader's interest).

Options

Generate a variety of possibilities before deciding what to do. When people bargain over positions they are, in effect, negotiating about moving up or down a scale. Should the target date be brought forward or put back? Is the price of the house too high or too low? Should the lease period be increased or reduced? There is a tendency to see the exercise in terms of winning or losing. If identified interests are to be satisfied then the parties need to set time aside during the negotiation to brainstorm possible ways of doing just that and then evaluating the options before deciding what they are actually going to do. The techniques involved are those described in Chapter 8. This problem-solving approach to negotiating is only possible if good working relationships have already been established and if agreement has been reached to treat the negotiation as a cooperative rather than as an adversarial exercise. This may not always be possible in negotiations between strangers or between different institutions, but should be feasible in those between project leaders and sponsors working in the same firm.

Criteria

The final element in the Harvard Negotiating Project's approach to principled negotiations is to insist that the result be based on objective criteria. If this is not done there is a danger of horse-trading. For instance, the project sponsor may say to the project leader, 'I went along with you on cost and deadlines and it is now your turn to go along with my wording of the project objective'. This is unsatisfactory. The outcome of each part of the negotiation needs to be based on principle rather than pressure. It is helpful for you to propose that your agreement be based on criteria such as professional standards, precedents, corporate values, scientific judgements, market values and equitable treatment. Clearly, getting agreement on the objective criteria against which the substantive outcomes may be judged is in itself a negotiation. You and the person with whom you are negotiating may find it difficult to agree on objective criteria. If so, one way of overcoming the problem is to ask a third party, someone you both regard as fair, to choose criteria that are appropriate to your situation. You are not asking that person to settle your substantive issue but rather to advise you on what standards to use to settle it.

In a negotiation between a project leader and a sponsor there may be precedents within the firm that provide guidance. These might include the amount of time that people typically give to part-time project work, the degree to which work can be subcontracted to outsiders and the ways in which information should be presented and communicated. It is helpful to base the negotiated results on such criteria to avoid outcomes being biased by pressure, the exploitation of power and contests of will.

You will have met the stakeholders' expectations if you and your team achieve the agreed objectives and the performance criteria. But this will not be the whole story. People have other expectations as well. When as clients we seek the service of a professional adviser, we are not only interested in that person's reputation for technical competence. We are also keen to know if we are likely to be kept fully informed regularly about progress, whether or not our adviser is going to be easy to contact, if we can expect jargon-free and easy-to-read documents and whether or not we can anticipate pleasant and comfortable interactions. In other words there are a number of less tangible service criteria that are important to us, as well as the reputation of the adviser for providing outstanding advice. It is exactly the same in project management. It is helpful to pay attention to the intangibles as well as the tangibles. A good starting point is to get an idea of the stakeholders' preferences for the ways that you and they will relate. You can do this by chatting and observing. For example, some stakeholders like to be kept informed about progress in writing. Others prefer a discussion. Some like details spelt out and others prefer a synopsis. Some only want to be kept informed if major changes or delays occur. Others like to be advised routinely on progress. Some prefer formal presentations and others welcome informal chats. Know your stakeholders' preferences and act accordingly. The success of your project may be just as dependent on meeting these sorts of expectations as achieving the formal objectives and performance criteria. Knowing the preferences of your stakeholders is at the core of building good working relationships.

If major changes such as a delay in completing the project become unavoidable then it is vital to inform the stakeholders at the earliest opportunity. It is helpful to bring expectations into line with reality. It is a bit like the difference between being kept informed about progress on a delayed aeroplane departure time and not being told. Neither situation is appealing but I get far more frustrated with the latter than the former. When I am told what the new take-off time is then my expectations change and I can do some shopping, go for a snack or read a book. When I am not told, I hang around and get irritated because I don't know what is happening. I find it difficult to make other arrangements. The important thing is to advise stakeholders of significant changes at the earliest opportunity and then keep them up to date about progress.

Of course, if you are lucky enough to exceed expectations with a project then not only will you and your team receive well-deserved plaudits but quite possibly your career will receive a boost as well. One way in which you can influence expectations, so that you stand a better chance of exceeding them, is not to over-promise and under-deliver. Some project leaders fall into the trap of promising to meet unrealistic deadlines in order to create a favourable early impression. It is usually prudent and more effective to do the reverse.

There are a couple of other points about communicating with stakeholders that are worth bearing in mind. For those of your stakeholders who wish to be kept informed about progress on a regular basis, a convenient way is to link communications with milestones or phased stages of project completion. Your communications could follow the review meetings that you have with the project team. The second point is that it is all too easy to forget to communicate when you are busy. If you really do not have the time to talk personally with the stakeholders or to write a report, then send them e-mails to reassure them that the project is going well. Tell them that you will be in touch with more detailed information within the next week. And then make sure that you do it!

TAKE ACTION TO DEAL WITH OPPOSITION TO THE PROJECT

You may find yourself managing a project and then discover, much to your surprise, that there is opposition to it in some parts of the firm. You are surprised because, after all, your sponsor is a senior figure, the project is clearly useful in your view and you have taken it for granted that everyone else goes along with the objectives and welcomes the work being done. However, since most projects are concerned with introducing change there may be individuals, and even teams, who prefer the status quo. If they have some power and influence they may try to oppose or even sabotage your efforts. If they are skilful politically they may do this covertly and you may be unaware of the dangers until too late. Good project leaders endeavour to anticipate opposition and, with the help of their sponsors, seek to satisfy the concerns of those involved. This means taking time at the start to think about who might oppose the project and why. Sometimes opponents can be reassured through discussions. On other occasions it may be necessary, with the agreement of the sponsor, to negotiate some changes to the objectives that will keep the project on track and take account of the worries and concerns of particular individuals and teams within the firm.

SELECT A PROJECT TEAM WITH A BALANCED MIX OF ATTRIBUTES

Sometimes you will be told who the members of your project team are going to be. That is generally unfortunate. It is much better if you can get your project sponsor to agree to you identifying and then inviting people of your choice to serve. If you are held accountable for a successful project outcome it seems reasonable that you should decide whom you want to help you to produce the results. If you are fortunate enough to make your own selection there are two things to bear in mind. It makes sense to have a mixture of people with the technical and commercial skills needed for the project. That is obvious enough. However, it is also helpful to have a group of individuals who make different contributions in terms of their temperaments. The concept of team roles, formulated by Dr Meredith Belbin (1981), was explored in Chapter 11 on selection. It is also helpful in project work. For example, some people are good at producing ideas. Others are good analysts. They ask questions and test understanding. Some people excel at taking on ideas and turning them into action. Some people are good at keeping the rest of the team on its toes. They remind people about deadlines and worry that all items on the agenda are covered properly. There are others who are good at mediating when conflicts arise and who excel at pouring oil on troubled waters. There are those who are good at representing the team with stakeholders and outsiders. There are yet others who provide energy and drive and help to keep up a high level of motivation among team members generally. So if you have the opportunity to identify a mixture of people to invite into the project team, try to achieve a balance of technical and commercial skills on the one hand and a mixture of creative, analytical, problem-solving, checking, caring, doing and shaping attributes on the other.

Part Five

Influencing skills

14

Influencing colleagues and clients

Example is not the main thing in influencing others.
It is the only thing.

— (Albert Schweitzer)

It is self-evident that the ability to influence others is a fundamental leadership attribute. Apart from their own team members, leaders sometimes need to influence colleagues, senior and junior, in other parts of the firm. They may need to represent the interests of the team with the senior management. Not least they have to be able to influence their clients. Coley Porter Bell provides product and packaging design, brand identity and new product development services to its clients. Chief Executive Cheryl Giovannoni highlights the importance of influencing skills:

> Our project team leaders have both an external and an internal role to play. It involves producing a synthesis of what the client wants and what the designers in the project team believe should be offered. This synthesis becomes the client firm's needs. This calls for a high level of influencing skill both outwards towards clients and inwards towards members of the team. To be able to

influence effectively, in my view, calls for a clear vision, openness and frankness, diplomacy, an ability to negotiate well – to give and take – and the avoidance of arrogance. With these professional and personal capabilities and a mature outlook it is possible to win the trust of both clients and team members. That is the mark of a good leader in our business.

The story is told of a woman who took her son to see Gandhi who asked what she wanted. 'I would like you to get him to stop eating sugar,' she replied. 'Bring the boy back in two weeks' time,' Gandhi replied. The woman returned with her son. Gandhi turned to the boy and said, 'Stop eating sugar'. The woman looked surprised and asked, 'Why did I have to wait two weeks for you to say that?' 'Two weeks ago I was eating sugar,' Gandhi replied. There are a number of useful skills to help the influencing process along. These are explored in this chapter. However, all the skills in the world are unlikely to compensate for personal behaviour that runs counter to the influence that we wish to bring to bear. In that sense, example is at the heart of our ability to influence others.

USE A RANGE OF INFLUENCING STYLES

You might like to try your hand at the influencing styles questionnaire in Figure 14.1 based on one originally designed by Roger Harrison and subsequently used extensively at Ashridge Business School. Answer each question by thinking about how you generally seek to influence your colleagues. As with all questionnaires that are concerned with behaviour, it is important to be as frank as possible so that a reasonably accurate picture emerges. Descriptions of the different influencing styles, also based on Roger Harrison's work, follow the questionnaire.

INFLUENCING STYLES QUESTIONNAIRE

Complete the score table, which appears after the questions, in the following way:

If you believe that the statement describes how you generally act, score 2.

If you believe that the statement describes how you occasionally act, score 1.

If you believe that you never act in the way described by the statement, score 0.

1. I do not hesitate to point out others' mistakes.

2. I am happy for others to undertake tasks even when there is a risk of my being personally criticized if they are not done well.

3. When others become uncertain or discouraged my enthusiasm carries them along.

4. I put forward lots of ideas and plans.

5. I am quick to praise or criticize other people's performance or behaviour.

6. I am willing to be influenced by others.

7. I can bring others to see the exciting possibilities in a situation.

8. I put together a good logical argument.

9. I articulate clear expectations that I think others ought to meet.

10. I encourage people to come up with their own solutions to problems.

11. My way of speaking conveys a sense of excitement to others.

12. When opposed I am quick to come forward with a counter-argument.

13. I let people know the standards by which I will judge their behaviour or performance.

14. I am receptive to the ideas and suggestions of others.

15. I communicate my belief in the value and importance of what my colleagues are doing.

16. I provide detailed plans on how things should be done.

17. I make moral judgements about what others do or say.

18. I am quick to admit my own mistakes.

19. I describe an exciting vision of what could be.

20. I suggest alternatives to the proposals that others have made.

21. I pass on praise and criticism that others have made about another's work.

22. I sympathize with others when they have difficulties.

23. My enthusiasm is contagious.

24. I push my ideas vigorously.

25. People can readily judge whether I approve or disapprove of what they do or say.

26. I listen to and try to use the ideas raised by others.

27. I am able to put into words the hopes, aspirations and fears that others may feel.

28. It is not unusual for me to stick my neck out with ideas and suggestions.

29. I use the power and authority I have to make others comply.

30. If others become angry or upset I listen with understanding.

31. I am skilful at using images and figures of speech to present exciting possibilities.

32. I put over my ideas clearly.

33. I let people know in advance what I expect of them.

34. I readily admit my lack of knowledge and expertise in a situation.

35. I help people become more aware of their strengths and potentialities that they have as a group.

36. I defend my own ideas energetically.

37. I offer bargains or deals to get what I want from others.

38. I put as much effort into developing the ideas of others as I do my own.

39. I am skilful in articulating the aims and goals that people have in common.

40. I anticipate objections to my point of view and am ready with a counter-argument.

41. I give frequent and specific feedback as to whether my expectations are being met.

42. I help others to get a hearing.

43. In seeking to persuade others I appeal to their values, emotions and feelings.

44. I frequently disregard the ideas of others in favour of my own proposals.

45. People always know whether or not they are measuring up to my standards.

46. I listen sympathetically to people who do not share my views.

47. I generate excitment and enthusiasm through my use of colourful language.

48. When other people disagree with my ideas, I don't give up but find other way to persuade them.

49. I make it clear what I am willing to give in return for what others want.

50. I am quite open about my hopes and fears, aspirations and personal difficulties in achieving them.

51. I foster an *esprit de corps* among my colleagues.

52. I am skilful at producing evidence in support of my own proposals.

53. I follow up the performance and behaviour of others to find out whether my expectations are being met.

54. I show tolerance and acceptance of others' feelings.

55. I use emotionally charged language to encourage enthusiasm for a task.

56. I talk about my own ideas more than I listen to those of others.

57. I give orders and instructions that I expect to be obeyed.

58. I accept criticism without becoming defensive.

59. I help others to see how they can achieve more by working together.

60. I present my ideas in an organized way.

61. I check up to see whether others are keeping their side of the bargain.

62. I help others to express themselves.

63. I help others to feel personally involved with and responsible for the future achievement of the group as a whole.

64. I draw attention to inconsistencies in the ideas of others.

65. I use rewards and punishments to make other people do what I want.

66. I go out of my way to show understanding of the needs and wants of others.

67. I strive to develop a sense of unity and common purpose among my colleagues.

68. It is not unusual for me to interrupt others while they are talking.

69. I judge people on what they do rather than what they say.

70. I don't pretend to be confident when I feel uncertain.

71. I try to excite interest by using metaphors and analogies when encouraging others to agree with me.

72. I put a lot of energy into arguing about what to do.

Enter the scores that you assign for each question in the space provided.

A	B	C	D
1 _____	2 _____	3 _____	4 _____
5 _____	6 _____	7 _____	8 _____
9 _____	10 _____	11 _____	12 _____
13 _____	14 _____	15 _____	16 _____
17 _____	18 _____	19 _____	20 _____
21 _____	22 _____	23 _____	24 _____
25 _____	26 _____	27 _____	28 _____
29 _____	30 _____	31 _____	32 _____
33 _____	34 _____	35 _____	36 _____
37 _____	38 _____	39 _____	40 _____
41 _____	42 _____	43 _____	44 _____
45 _____	46 _____	47 _____	48 _____
49 _____	50 _____	51 _____	52 _____
53 _____	54 _____	55 _____	56 _____
57 _____	58 _____	59 _____	60 _____
61 _____	62 _____	63 _____	64 _____
65 _____	66 _____	67 _____	68 _____
69 _____	70 _____	71 _____	72 _____

TOTALS

Figure 14.1   Influencing styles questionnaire

DESCRIPTIONS OF THE FOUR STYLES REVEALED BY THE QUESTIONNAIRE

Assertive persuasion

This style is characterized by the use of logic, facts and opinions to persuade others. Individuals who are effective at using this style make good proposals and suggestions about what to do and how to do it. They are not afraid to stick their necks out and submit their ideas to the test of other people's reactions. They are skilful in marshalling evidence and arguments in support of their proposals and in rebutting those with which they disagree. They are persistent and energetic in persuading others. Sometimes they may not listen very well to the points others raise or they may listen only to find weaknesses in the opinions expressed.

An emphasis on logical argument as opposed to an appeal to emotions is a prime characteristic of this style. People who use it well are usually very articulate and participate actively in discussions and arguments about ideas, plans and proposals. They enjoy the cut and thrust of debate and even when they are defending an inferior position they may battle away with enthusiasm and determination.

Rewards and punishments

This style is characterized by the use of pressures and incentives to try to control the behaviour of others. It may take the form of offering rewards for compliance or of threatening with punishment or deprivation for non-compliance. It may involve the use of naked power or more indirect and veiled pressures exerted through the possession of status, prestige and formal authority. There is liberal use of praise and criticism, approval and disapproval and moralistic judgements of right and wrong.

People who use **rewards and punishments** go out of their way to let others know what they want, expect or require of them and what standards will be used in judging their performance. They then follow up to find out what has been done and give approval or disapproval, praise or blame, rewards or punishments accordingly. They tend to be specific and detailed in communicating their requirements and they follow up quickly with the positive and negative incentives. Psychologists say that the effective use of this style involves much heavier use of praise than criticism. Many who use the style, however, do not follow this dictum and they are frequently more negative than positive.

An important aspect of using rewards and punishments is the 'management of contingencies', which means communicating clearly to others what they must do in order to get what they want and to avoid negative consequences. Traditional bargaining, involving the use of offers and counter-offers and threats and counter-threats, is a good example of this process. If you let others know what you will do to or for them if they do or don't do such and such, you are engaged in 'contingency management'. Niccolo Machiavelli's book *The Prince* portrays 'contingency management' on a grand scale (1999).

In using both rewards and punishments and **assertive persuasion** you may agree or disagree with others and approve or disapprove of their ideas and actions. The difference is in what backs up the agreement or disagreement and approval or disapproval. In assertive persuasion you may agree or disagree because of your judgement of the rationality of the other person's position or because you think it is more or less effective, correct, accurate or true. The ultimate appeal is to reason, logic and reality. In using rewards and punishments, on the other hand, the judgement of right and wrong does not depend on rationality. The standard is external to the person being judged, for example a moral or social standard, a regulation or a performance standard. It is the compliance or not with this external standard that causes the evaluation of right or wrong or good or bad.

In practice, the best way to tell the difference is to note whether the judgement is given with or without a reason. If it is merely 'That's right' or 'You're wrong', then it is likely that the person is using the rewards and punishments style. If a reason is given, it is more likely that assertive persuasion is being used.

Participation and trust

The efficacy of this style depends on involving others in decision-making and problem-solving processes. When others can be induced to take an active part in making a decision their commitment to carry it out is increased and the amount of follow-up required is markedly reduced. The person being influenced contributes his or her energy to the work, and the amount of effort required from the influencer is therefore reduced. Thus, whereas the **assertive persuasion** and **rewards and punishments** styles may be thought of as 'pushing' others to do what is required, **participation and trust** involves drawing or 'pulling' others in to decide and act.

If others are to be actively involved they should feel that they have the resources required for the task, that their contributions are received and understood and that their efforts are valued. An atmosphere of mutual trust and cooperation is conducive to participation. People are helped to contribute when they believe that others will not belittle or ignore their contributions and when there is an atmosphere of openness and non-defensiveness. In short, participation is encouraged by receptivity, understanding and openness and is discouraged by attempting to gain control over others or by competitively trying to win one's own points.

People who rely a good deal on participation and trust tend to listen well, drawing out contributions from others and showing understanding and appreciation when contributions are forthcoming.

They do a lot of building on, and extending, the ideas of others rather than pushing their own proposals. They are quick to give credit to others for their contributions. Rather than counter-attacking when their own ideas and proposals are questioned, people who use this style tend to be open and non-defensive about their own limitations. They do not put up a strong front to hide their own weaknesses. By their example they try to create trust and openness in relationships, so that others feel accepted for what they are and do not feel the need to compete for attention and control.

Common vision

This style involves identifying and articulating a common or shared vision of what the future of an organization, group or team could be. It is concerned with strengthening the members' beliefs that the desired outcomes can be achieved through their individual and collective efforts.

The **common vision** style involves mobilizing the energy and resources of others through appeals to their hopes, values and aspirations. It also works through activating the feelings of strength and confidence that are generated by being part of a group with a shared common purpose.

Common vision shares with **assertive persuasion** an emphasis on the ability to present ideas orally. It differs in that the appeal is not primarily to the intellect but rather to emotions and values held by the recipient. Further, the attempt is not so much to inject energy and enthusiasm into others as it is to activate the commitment and strength that are bound up in their hopes, aspirations and ideals and to channel that energy into work and problem solving.

Typical of the skills possessed by people who use common vision effectively is the ability to see and to articulate to others the exciting possibilities that exist in an idea or an assignment and to project these possibilities enthusiastically. The skilled practitioner uses images and metaphors to kindle enthusiasm about a better future. The leader using the common vision style helps others to identify the values, hopes and aspirations that they have in common and to feel the strength in unity found in cohesive groups. The leader emphasizes what he or she and the group can do together. Stress is placed, for example, on 'what we can accomplish to make a better future for all of us if we work together to achieve common goals and ideals'. Charismatic leaders like Sir Winston Churchill and John Kennedy used a lot of common vision. So did others like Hitler and Mussolini. The common vision style can be used to pursue high ideals and worthy goals or, on the other hand, to foster support for dangerous intentions and narrow, selfish ends.

INTERPRET THE RESULTS

It will be apparent to you by now that your column A score reflects the extent to which you use the rewards and punishments style. Columns B, C and D, respectively, represent the participation and trust, common vision and assertive persuasion styles. Some people use all four styles to a greater or lesser degree whilst others are more inclined to stick primarily to one or two styles. A case can be made for leaders of professional service teams to become competent at using all four styles. We saw in Chapter 2 that good leaders are able to communicate a sense of direction, goals and values. Clearly the common vision style of influencing is helpful for this purpose. We also saw that effective leaders empower their team members in the achievement of day-to-day tasks and in the implementation of the team's strategy. The participation and trust influencing style is tailor-made for this purpose. We saw in Chapter 6 on motivation that recognition for good performance is important. In other words this is the 'rewards' side of the rewards and punishment style. We have seen that negative incentives occasionally have to be used but preferably as a last resort. They may be used as part of a disciplinary procedure when all other positive efforts to change behaviour or improve performance have failed. Finally, assertive persuasion can be a very useful influencing style to use with others who enjoy and expect the cut and thrust of debate and who like logical and rational arguments. Many lawyers, especially those engaged in litigation and advocacy, use this style to great effect. It is often expected by those with whom they have to deal. It is a mode of behaviour that is commonplace within some institutions and for particular business and professional purposes. However, if used as a way of influencing people who may be intimidated by powerful logical arguments it can produce disastrous results. Assertive persuaders can win the argument but completely fail to influence those who need, and expect, an appeal to the heart as well as to the mind. They may be admired for the logic with which they present their views yet at the same time fail to influence those who expect and prefer to be involved in the decision-making process. I have seen very capable professionals use assertive persuasion to great effect with some of their senior colleagues or with representatives of other firms. I have seen the same people completely fail to carry other colleagues by using the same style in circumstances when using participation and trust would have quite probably produced much better results.

Successful leaders are likely to be versatile enough to be able to use each of the four styles depending on the circumstances in which they find themselves. The effective use of rewards and punishments and participation and trust styles depends, largely, on a willingness to behave in the ways required. It is primarily a matter of attitude. To be good at the common vision style requires, among other things, an ability to speak in an exciting and colourful way to groups of people. This comes naturally to some but others may need some guidance and practice with feedback. The assertive persuasion style involves the use of good debating skills and the ability to think quickly on one's feet. Again these come naturally to some but others may need to seek advice and school themselves in the arts involved.

FOCUS ON PROBLEMS BEFORE SOLUTIONS WHEN HELPING OTHERS

We are all familiar with the skills that a good medical general practitioner uses when a patient arrives at the surgery with a physical ailment. The doctor begins by getting on the right wavelength and establishing rapport. This is followed by questions to help to understand the problem and make a diagnosis. Only after concentrating on the matter in this way does the doctor offer possible solutions.

Following a similar process can be helpful when we are seeking to influence team colleagues or clients. Sometimes, however, in our haste to resolve issues and take action we move to solutions too rapidly and as a result produce inadequate or even wrong answers. Dick McCann in his book *How to Influence Others at Work* (1988) has produced a straightforward and effective model to assist us to concentrate on problems before arriving at solutions when helping others. The model is shown in Figure 14.2, and an examination of its component parts follows.

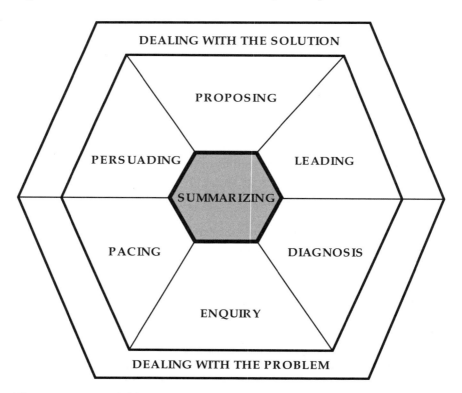

Figure 14.2   Model for helping others to solve problems

Pacing

This is getting on the right wavelength and establishing rapport with those to be influenced. Useful techniques include:

▌ Talking on neutral subjects, or small talk, to test the ground and relationships, for instance weather, sport, television programmes and traffic congestion.

▌ Adjusting behaviour to that of the person being influenced. This is known as mirroring. For example, voice tempo and tone can be modified to come some way towards that of the other person. If he talks quickly then you adjust your speed accordingly to some degree. If she talks slowly then you do likewise. This has to be done with care, of course, to avoid mimicry. If she is full of enthusiasm and you are laid back try to step up the pace, but only to a degree. It can also be helpful to mirror physical behaviour. For instance, rapport is more likely if you stand when the other person is standing. Leaning slightly towards someone who is leaning towards you is preferable to leaning away if you want to be on the same wavelength. This happens naturally with people who are comfortable with each other. If necessary it can be contrived, to a degree, with positive results. But don't overdo it!

▌ If you need to influence people who are agitated or fed up then use either 'feeling-facts' or 'fact-feelings' loops during the pacing phase. For instance, suppose that you have someone working for you who is under pressure to produce a draft of the team's business plan by the end of the week. You need to talk to her to change some basic assumptions a day before her deadline. She is agitated and angry, as a result, and you need to calm her before getting down to business. Using a 'feeling–facts loop' is a useful way to cope with the problem. See Figure 14.3.

▌ As you can see you start with a 'feeling statement' and, in quick succession, mention three relevant and pertinent facts and then back to a 'feeling statement'. You demonstrate your sympathy with her annoyance and back that sympathy up with appropriate facts. Starting and finishing with a 'feeling statement' helps to calm her down.

Contrast this with the need to influence a person who is feeling low and fed up. This time the requirement at the pacing stage is to 'lift the spirits' before getting down to business. This time you use a

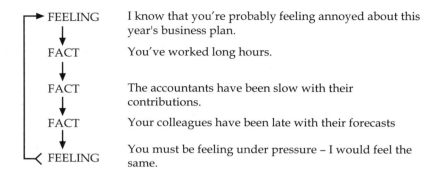

Figure 14.3 Feeling–Facts Loop

'fact–feelings loop'. Suppose that you have a designer working for you who has done a first-class piece of work on a proposal but the assignment has been lost to a competitor. See Figure 14.4.

In this case you start with a 'fact statement' and, in quick succession, back it up with three relevant and appropriate 'feeling statements' and then back to a 'fact statement'. You demonstrate that good work was done and support that fact with feelings of sympathy over the lost business. Starting and finishing with a 'fact statement' helps to lift his spirits when the fact represents good news.

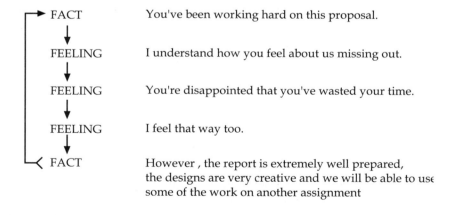

Figure 14.4 Fact–feelings loop

Enquiry

It is advantageous when influencing others to distinguish between those parts of the discussion that relate to the problem and those parts that relate to the solution. Problem enquiry is a way of helping the other person to explore all of the possibilities surrounding an issue and to bring out information that might be useful in the resolution of the problem. It is important to try to see through the smokescreens, misunderstandings and differing perceptions that may cloud the matter. Questioning technique is important. The use of 'softeners', which are questions that take the edge off stark interrogating styles, is helpful during the early phases of the enquiry stage. Questions like 'To what extent do you think . . . ?', 'I wonder whether . . . ?' and 'Do you think it would be useful if . . . ?' are helpful 'softeners'. Another technique to soften the interrogative style is to intersperse factual enquiries with feeling enquiries.

Having said that, there is no doubt that questions that begin with the interrogatives 'what', 'where', 'when', 'why', 'how' and 'who' tend to provide more useful answers than questions that begin with verbs, such as 'Do you . . . ?', 'Can you . . . ?', 'Will you . . . ?' and 'Have you . . . ?'

During the enquiry phase it is important to check for generalizations, incomplete arguments, mind reading, unjustified sweeping statements and implied cause and effect. Here are some examples:

▌ *Generalization* – 'Something should be done to rectify the situation.'
Questions to obtain clarification – What should be done? What situation are you referring to?

▌ *Incomplete argument* – 'The programmers claim that they have been victimized.'
Questions to obtain clarification – Who do they consider is victimizing them? To whom are they claiming victimization?

▌ *Mind reading* – 'Everybody in this team is waiting for Jim to cock it up.'
Questions to obtain clarification – How did you discover that? How do you know that?

▌ *Unjustified sweeping statement* – 'People should avoid conflict.'
Questions to obtain clarification – What would happen if you had to confront conflict?
What do you believe is the eventual outcome of sweeping conflict under the carpet?

▌ *Implied cause and effect* – 'I would like to do a good job on this project but I don't have the time.'

 Questions to obtain clarification – If you had the time would you be able to do it?

 Why is time a problem for you?

Diagnosis

The third stage is to undertake the diagnosis. This is to identify the cause of the problem. In its simplest form a diagnosis indicates the cause or reason for something occurring. It is a good idea to help the person being influenced to arrive at her or his own diagnosis. Successful self-analysis generally encourages a greater willingness to resolve the problem and take appropriate action.

Leading

Use questions that lead the person being influenced to work towards his or her own solutions. Use questions like:

▌ 'How could you do that differently?'

▌ 'What could you do more of?'

▌ 'What could you do less of?'

▌ 'How can your project be completed on time?'

▌ 'What can you do to prevent this from happening again?'

When appropriate, use examples, stories and illustrations from your own experience that are relevant to the problem to help the process along. As at the diagnosis stage, it is beneficial, for similar reasons of ownership and commitment, to help the person being influenced to come up with his or her own solution.

Proposing

If you fail to get the person being influenced to arrive at a solution than it may be necessary to make some proposals to help the problem to be resolved. You are more likely to exercise influence if you have gone through all of the earlier stages described than if you jump straight into the proposal phase. It is better, also, to prefix your proposals with a 'softener' phrase. For example:

▌ 'I think that perhaps you should consider . . . '

▌ 'I suggest that . . . '

▌ 'It might be a good idea if . . . '

▌ 'You might like to . . . '

▌ 'How about . . . ?'

▌ 'It seems to me that a good way forward would be . . . '

Another effective way is to frame proposals in question format: 'Are you able to talk to the meeting on Tuesday, please?' or 'Can you have this report written by next Wednesday, please?'

Persuading

Generally speaking, techniques of persuading should only be used after sufficient time has been spent on the other phases. Persuading sometimes becomes necessary if the person being influenced has not managed, with your help, to come up with a solution to the problem. It is also a useful device for removing any seeds of doubt as to whether the right decision has already been made. It is a particularly good skill to use when seeking to influence a group of people. Useful techniques for persuading others include:

▌ Use colourful illustrations, stories, metaphors and analogies. We have already seen in Chapter 5 on communications that it is a good idea, however, to avoid old, overused metaphors, which tend to be boring clichés. Original metaphors, however, work. They draw attention to the relationships of ideas, images and symbols. Good and original metaphors give two ideas for one. They help to simplify complicated issues. They capture the imagination.

▌ Use sensory-based words. People's interpretations of the world, ideas and events are partly influenced by their senses of sight, sound, touch and smell. Most of us find that our interpretations are helped by one of the sensory channels rather more than by the others. For example, the word 'snow' will summon up distinct sensory experiences in the imagination and thought processes of different people. Some will see in their imagination 'a beautiful snow-clad mountain on a sunny day'; others will almost feel 'the exuberance of skiing down a steep slope'; some may virtually hear 'the squeals of joy as young children throw snowballs'; and yet others will all but smell 'the crisp early morning air'. Of course the sensory images may be quite different, such as 'seeing oneself struggling through a blizzard'; or 'feeling cold feet and hands'; or 'hearing the swish of cars moving through the slush'; or 'smelling a sodden pet dog'.

When trying to persuade others it is useful to choose words that will help people to paint pictures in their minds of events yet to occur; to judge circumstances by evoking memories through sound; or to evaluate situations in terms of their feelings. To cope with the range of individual preferences it is helpful to use sensory saturation. It means appealing to a number of the sensory channels, rather than just one, especially when trying to persuade a group of people to accept a point of view. It involves sprinkling conversations and presentations with a variety of sensory-based words and phrases. Here are a few examples of visual words: 'look', 'see', 'notice', 'reveal', 'reflect', 'examine' and 'insight'. Possible visual phrases are: 'I see what you mean'; 'we see eye to eye'; 'beyond a shadow of doubt'; and 'that will shed some light on the matter'. Auditory words include 'say', 'tone', 'resonate', 'ring', 'dissonant' and 'harmonious'. Auditory phrases include 'on the same wavelength'; 'rings a bell'; 'loud and clear'; and 'music to my ears'. Feeling words include 'touch', 'warm', 'heavy', 'grasp', 'suffer' and 'tangible'. Feeling phrases include 'I can grasp that idea'; 'I can't put my finger on it'; 'scratch the surface'; and 'firm foundation'. Sensory saturation is frequently used in television advertisements. It is instructive to analyse them in terms of the sensory channels to which they are appealing.

▌ Use 'fat' words (ostentatious diction). Fat words, expressed enthusiastically, can be helpful in persuading and motivating others. These words, often strong on rhetoric and rather weaker on substance, such as 'lifestyle', 'epoch-making', 'loyalty', 'dream', 'spirit', 'beacon' and 'liberty', can be effective when seeking to persuade groups of people, for instance in meetings. They are useful, also, to help to get commitment at the end of a conversation or talk, the rest of which may have been more measured in terms of the words used. They are less effective, however, in the written form or in one-to-one encounters.

▌ Use implied cause-and-effect relationships and express them with enthusiasm. This approach is best demonstrated by the use of example statements:

– 'When you attend this workshop you will feel that you have done the right thing.'
– 'Just seeing the car in action will make you want to buy.'
– 'As you read the book you will realize that the ideas expressed will help you in your day-to-day leadership.'
– 'As we watched the demonstration of the software package we could immediately see the benefits for our business.'

Summarizing

Summarizing is shown in the centre of the model. It is so positioned because summarizing can and should be used, at several stages, during both problem analysis and generating solutions. Summarizing statements help to tie the fragments of a conversation together. They also allow for checking, that there is mutual understanding, that both individuals are travelling on the same road and that there is agreement up to the point of the summary. Frequent summarizing is especially important when there is conflict over goals or interests.

THINK THROUGH A STRATEGY FOR INFLUENCING OTHERS TO ACCEPT IDEAS FOR CHANGE

When you wish to influence your colleagues, especially those in senior positions, to accept your ideas, or those of your team, for changes to policies, processes or working practices, you are more likely to succeed if you think about tackling the problem in a systematic way. Here are some suggested steps that you might take when seeking to influence others:

▌ Be clear about the reasons for the proposed change. Identify and spell out the benefits to the firm and to your colleagues of the change that you have in mind.

▌ Consider the forces in favour and those against the change. Weight the stronger forces more heavily than the weaker ones and form a judgement about the ease or difficulty of convincing your colleagues of the change that you desire. Assess what needs to be done to make the change happen and set objectives.

▌ Identify the network of individuals and groups affected by the change and the risks and opportunities for them of being involved. Identify the individuals and groups whose cooperation will be essential for the change to be brought to a successful conclusion. Decide if you need to work with them to bring influence to bear. Identify those who might resist or oppose the change and ascertain why and to what extent. Decide how you will reduce or overcome the resistance or opposition.

▌ Assess your relationships in terms of trust with those to be influenced, those whose support is required and those who will oppose you. Decide on the different approaches and styles needed to deal with them. Take account of their positions, power and personalities.

▌ Prepare contingency options to your proposed change in case of failure.

▌ Prepare a timetable for each stage of the change process

PLAY YOUR PART
IN INFLUENCING THE FIRM'S CULTURE

We saw in Chapter 4 that team leaders throughout the firm have a part to play in bringing about the desired culture. It is not only a matter for those in senior positions. The values of the firm will not be actively embraced unless leaders of all teams reinforce them at every opportunity. Here are some simple ways for team leaders to influence the cultures of their firms:

▌ Behave as a role model and set examples to others. If attending meetings on time is regarded as desirable conduct then make sure that you are always there a few minutes before the start.

▌ Engage in lots of talk with your team members. Discuss goals and the ways of meeting them with your colleagues both one to one and with the team as a whole.

▌ Commit the main values, beliefs and standards of conduct to writing and circulate the information in a simple and colourful way to your team colleagues.

▌ Reinforce beliefs with standards and rewards. If the firm believes in outstanding service quality then agree quality standards and reward those who achieve them. If the firm believes that people should invest time in learning then agree standards and reward those who develop their skills.

▌ When you recruit new team members select those who fit the desired culture or who are clearly capable of adapting to it.

▌ When you promote people make sure that they embody the desired culture.

▌ Ensure that the coaching and mentoring that you do is concerned with the firm's philosophy, values and beliefs as well as with skills, methods and techniques.

▌ Create events, for example workshops, at which you and your team colleagues explore values and beliefs and the ways that they can be 'lived' on a day-to-day basis.

Part Six

Common leadership problems

15

Leadership exercises

PROBLEMS

Here are a few leadership problems for you to think about. You should assume that you are the team leader in each of the problems posed. What do you think that you should do?

1.   You have asked a trainee in your team to draft a document. She has had some experience of similar work before. The draft is submitted for your approval, by agreement, two working days before it is due to be sent to the client. There are a number of problems with the way that it is written. What do you do and what do you say to the trainee?

2.   There are four secretaries in your team and morale is on the low side because they feel uninvolved. This is the message that has come to you via two of the people in your department. Currently you invite the secretaries to all meetings. They always turn up but only contribute on the rare occasion when you invite their comments on administrative matters. What can you do to improve the situation?

3.   You have an ambitious member of your team who would like to become a partner in due course. He is very competent technically and has excellent people skills. You believe that he has leadership potentiality and that he will be a considerable asset to the firm. However, he dislikes selling the firm's services. He feels that it is a rather unsavoury activity and he believes that business should be generated by word of mouth based on outstanding service. This dislike of selling will hold him back in your view. What can you do about the situation?

RECOMMENDED SOLUTIONS

These are my answers to the problems. You might like to compare them with your views. In practice solutions are bound to vary a bit depending on the culture of the firm and the values of the people involved.

1. This is an opportunity to do some coaching. The easiest and quickest thing to do would be to go through the draft with a red pen and correct it in the manner that appeals and hand it back. Another way, only slightly better, would be to describe to the trainee how you believe the document should be drafted and give your reasons. However, I believe that you will achieve far more lasting benefits by having a discussion along the following lines. You could ask the trainee how particular sentences and paragraphs might be reworded. In the process you could encourage the use of short sentences and readily understood words. In this way you will help to raise awareness and encourage the trainee to accept responsibility for improving her drafting skills.

2. It is helpful for secretaries to attend at least some team meetings. They are important members of the team and if they are always left out then they are likely to be demoralized. However, they are also likely to be dissatisfied if they are required to waste their time by attending meetings that have little or no bearing on their work and where they find it difficult to make a useful contribution. For people to contribute effectively they need to feel that they are deriving some benefits. The answer is to plan meetings carefully and involve secretaries when there are issues on the agenda for which they are likely to be willing to make a contribution. Make sure that these occur at fairly regular intervals.

3. He has excellent people skills. It should be quite easy for him, therefore, to develop his ability to sell. It is a question of attitude and motivation. My recommendation is for you to do some personal counselling about the value to the firm and to his career if he develops his competence to sell services. You could follow up by having discussions about the selling process and re-emphasizing the importance of the selling activity. Stress the fact that to be a partner he needs to be good technically, to have leadership potentiality and to be able to generate new business. Give him the opportunity to shadow a good sales person. Finally, encourage him to have a go. Give him some constructive feedback on how he has done.

PROBLEMS

4.   A young person in a sub-group in your team is an excellent per-former and she is highly motivated. She is a great asset to the firm and would be a considerable loss if she left. She could get another job easily. She has complained to you that her boss is a 'control freak' who over-manages her in every way. He asks for daily reports on progress on lengthy assignments. He checks all work, including letters, despite never finding any problems. He fails to let her take technical decisions without first checking with him. What changes in leadership style should he make and what should you do to facilitate appropriate changes in his behaviour?

5.   You have decided that your team members need to improve service quality. They meet the generally accepted firm-wide quality stan-dards but you believe that, for competitive reasons, service quality needs to be offered at a much higher level in your team. How can you get your team to generate and then implement good ideas for exceeding expectations and delighting the clients?

6.   A young member of your team is very well informed and highly motivated. The quality of his work is excellent. However, he lacks confidence to take decisions on his own. He always seeks you out to check that his decisions, drafted documents, letters etc are satisfacto-ry. He also checks with you before making telephone calls to clients to check that what he is going to say is correct. Invariably he is on the right lines. What can you do to boost his confidence and encourage him to take more responsibility for his own actions?

RECOMMENDED SOLUTIONS

4. The team leader who reports to you should be counselled. My approach would be to discuss in detail the different leadership styles that are appropriate depending on whether or not people are fully skilled to undertake their tasks and motivated to perform well. In this case the team member is excellent at her job and is highly motivated. The surest way of demoralizing her, as appears to be the case, is to over-control. You should counsel the team leader to 'let go' a bit. Emphasize that it might well be appropriate to monitor performance regularly, and in detail, with less accomplished performers. In this case there is little risk, and everything to be gained for both the team leader and the person concerned, in leading with a light touch. The team member will enjoy and benefit from having the autonomy and the team leader will have more time for other things.

5. Here is an opportunity for the team collectively to do some brainstorming, evaluate the ideas generated and then agree on the specific actions to be taken to enhance service quality. A team meeting set up for this task, preferably in a relaxed environment away from the office, would probably produce two benefits. First of all, some good ideas capable of being implemented would be produced and, secondly, if well run the event would contribute to the development of team cohesion. The team leader's responsibility is to set the meeting up and to ensure that agreed action points are subsequently implemented. You may wish to facilitate the brainstorming and decision making or you may prefer to ask a colleague who would be good at the task and would enjoy it to do it instead.

6. There are some good performers, often young, who nevertheless lack confidence to take decisions about their day-to-day work without checking that they are on the right lines. I have two suggestions. First, give plenty of positive feedback and praise for the high-quality work already undertaken. It is important to be specific rather than general. Secondly, you and the person concerned could agree on issues that do not need to be checked before action. The number of matters falling into the checkable category will diminish, by agreement, over time. In this way the team member will progressively take more responsibility for his own actions and develop confidence. It is important nevertheless for you to offer a genuine lifeline. Keep your door open and be available if needed.

PROBLEMS

7. There have been several complaints recently that when team members cannot be contacted it is difficult to get anyone else to help with the query. Clients have to wait for several days, on occasions, to get their queries answered. What changes can be instituted to deal with these problems and how will you get your team members to implement the changes?

8. One of your team is very competent technically, a good sales person and an excellent team player. She provides support very readily whenever her colleagues need it. Her main weakness is an inability to prioritize work in terms of what is important. As a result she spends her life under the pressure of deadlines, many self-imposed. How can you help her? What do you say to her? What questions do you ask? What performance improvements should you try to agree? What will you do to turn good intentions into effect?

9. Your own boss is autocratic, abrupt and peremptory and inclined to lead and manage through the issuing of orders. This behaviour is, in your view, counter to the firm's culture as well as being an anathema to you personally. You know that you have a reputation as an effective performer. Should you put up with this and, if not, what is the appropriate way for you to deal with the situation?

RECOMMENDED SOLUTIONS

7.   It is important when new working practices are established that there is commitment from all team members for implementation. A good way to ensure that this happens is to involve your colleagues in the process of thinking through solutions. A brainstorming session for this purpose can be held and agreement sought on the actions to be taken. Whatever answers to the problem are evolved they are likely to include mechanisms to ensure that clients are contacted within a very few hours by the team member responsible. If that is impossible, because of long-term absence such as illness or holidays, then another colleague will always be available to hold the fort. Once procedures are agreed it is helpful for you to monitor performance by checking periodically that the new methods are working. Any evidence of team members not taking action must be taken up with them at once. In professional work, clients are often lost because of a failure to address these sorts of service issues even when the technical work is first class.

8.   This is another opportunity to do some coaching. In my view the main aim will be to help her to raise her awareness about the cause of always feeling under pressure. It is primarily because she leaves important tasks until too close to their deadlines. A combination of questions, and your own thoughts, will help her to understand the cause of the difficulty. Once that is clear you could help her, for a time, to plan her work so that the important tasks are undertaken with time to spare before target dates. She should then be able to see how urgent matters that arise can be fitted in more easily to the work schedule. As time passes you can encourage her to take full responsibility for planning her work. Subsequent periodic chats to see how things are progressing and to demonstrate your support will be helpful.

9.   You should certainly not put up with this state of affairs. The type of boss that you have is not very likely to welcome feedback. However, I believe that the first thing that you should try to do is to convey to him that his behaviour is unhelpful and counter-productive. It affects your morale and performance. Even with the most difficult people, feedback sometimes works. Some people go through life leaving a trail of damage behind them without being aware because nobody has told them. If this approach fails then seek a meeting with a senior member of the firm whom you judge to be sympathetic and who has the clout to do something about the problem. Explain the difficulty and mention that you have already sought to resolve it by talking to the person concerned.

PROBLEMS

10. Your team members are very individualistic and fail to give each other support. They are not inclined to field queries for colleagues who are away from their desks. They do not share the benefits of their knowledge and skills with colleagues even when that would enhance team performance. They dislike meetings, with the result that they fail to contribute enthusiastically. They like to keep their colleagues away from their own clients. How can you foster team spirit and behaviour? What should you do and how will you implement the needed changes?

11. You have heard, via the grapevine, that you are not as adept as you might be at letting your team know about the performance of the firm and the team and about major changes due to take place. Your team members complain to their colleagues elsewhere in the firm that they are unclear about the team's objectives. What should you do?

12. Two of your team members clearly dislike each other very much on a personal basis. They are both highly competent in their own spheres of work but don't cooperate with each other when faced with the need to run seminars or make presentations to potential clients. They oppose each other's views at team meetings. You have the impression that they do this due to a personality clash rather than because they feel strongly about the issues. Although their work is good on an individual basis, their behaviour towards each other is dysfunctional. It irritates other team members and distracts the team from best efforts. What should you do to resolve the situation?

RECOMMENDED SOLUTIONS

10. Fostering team spirit and mutual support is one of the more fundamental leadership activities. It is especially important in professional service work. Professionals tend to guard their independence and may become, as a consequence, ill-disciplined team players. A useful way to foster good teamwork is to agree a basic code of behaviour. Given that your people do not like meetings you will need to take great care in setting this session up. You will need to provide cogent reasons for your belief that having a strong and integrated team can help your collective performance. That is good for business and for attracting and retaining good individual performers. It might be useful to use an external facilitator, with no axe to grind, to run the session. The code of behaviour that your team develops is likely to cover such matters as attendance at meetings, collective responsibility for decisions, helping each other, sharing knowledge, support for each other, collective reviews of team performance, honouring commitments, exploration of new ideas, resolving conflicts and handling complaints.

11. I believe that you will enhance your reputation by being absolutely straight with your team members. Tell them that you have picked up some criticisms of your leadership performance on the grapevine and apologize. Tell them that you fully understand the importance of keeping them informed about the firm's progress, the team's performance and major changes. Ask them for some feedback and explore with them appropriate simple processes for communicating information and agreeing team objectives in the future.

12. A good way to deal with this problem is for you to put on your mediator's hat. Describe the conflict and its effects. Ask each person to comment on the causes of disagreement as they see them. Ask each person to summarize what has been said to demonstrate understanding. Ask each person in turn to spell out points of agreement and disagreement. Finally, invite them to suggest actions to capitalize on the points of agreement and to overcome the disagreements. This cooperative problem-solving approach may not guarantee a complete resolution of the issue but it is likely to help progress and achieve some positive results. Problems of this sort should be tackled as soon as they become evident. If they are left to fester, the demoralizing impact on the team as a whole is magnified hugely.

PROBLEMS

13. You know that as a team leader you are very good at one-to-one activities. You coach and consult well and you keep people informed regularly. You always have time for people and you are very willing to help them with technical and other problems. However, you are very uncomfortable with running team meetings and making presentations to groups of colleagues and clients. Whenever possible you avoid these activities and try to deal with issues instead on a one-to-one basis. You realize that this is sometimes inappropriate and time-consuming. What can you do to develop your skills and confidence to make presentations and run meetings?

14. You have a partner in your team who is an outstanding fee earner. He always exceeds his annual target. He works alone and generates his own business. However, he does not participate in any of the team activities. He avoids meetings; he does not contribute to brainstorming sessions; he refuses to supervise the work of trainees; he doesn't field queries for absent colleagues; and he resents any attempt by you to get him involved in broader team issues. What should you do?

15. You have a team member who is excellent at generating new business, keeping clients informed, meeting deadlines, contributing to teamwork, billing, running seminars and writing articles. She is a little careless with her technical work, however. She fails, on occasions, to check facts before committing information to paper. In the last year, errors have come to light, none of them too significant, but all nevertheless potentially embarrassing for the firm. You spoke to her when each of these errors was discovered. You feel that you must now try to ensure that she avoids a repetition of these problems. How can you help her to avoid errors in the future whilst at the same time ensuring that her enthusiasm and abilities remain intact?

RECOMMENDED SOLUTIONS

13. It is essential for team leaders to be competent in both one-to-one and group situations. Whilst some people who have a flair for making presentations and running meetings will invariably do a first-class job it is possible for all of us to improve our skills. The simple answer to this problem is for you to undertake training to help to raise confidence. Choose courses that provide an opportunity to try the new skills out and at which you get feedback and receive video-recording playbacks. Subsequently get one or two colleagues to give you feedback following presentations and meetings.

14. It is not uncommon for this sort of 'prima donna', who is not a team player, to be let off the hook. Everyone just accepts that he is going to do his own thing and excuses are made for him. I believe that this is wrong. Very often the damaging effects on other team members eventually outweigh the benefits that accrue from individual 'star' performance. It is possible for people to change their behaviour. It is worth while, therefore, for you to try to bring this about. The first step is for you to describe the behaviour that is undesirable. Then explain why you are concerned and why you think it would be helpful if there were to be a change. Ask him for the reasons for the unsatisfactory behaviour. Help him to see how a change will help his career and his relationships with his colleagues. Finally, invite his ideas on what can be done and agree a plan of action. If none of this works then I believe that you should seriously consider whether he should remain with you. Indulging one individual, however technically brilliant, will foster resentment and, in the long run, may damage team performance.

15. This is another opportunity for coaching. You need to get to the bottom of why the mistakes are occurring. Again good questions are the basis for raising awareness. If it turns out that she is careless with her technical work because of genuine time pressures then perhaps for the time being it will be helpful for her to cut back a little on other activities like running seminars and writing articles. On the other hand it may become evident that the carelessness is due to not bothering to check. If so you could instigate a speedy joint review process before work goes out. You need to stress the importance of accurate information. You could also add that you will be happy to drop the review process once things are back on an even keel. Give positive feedback about her other accomplishments. Encourage her to see that first-class performance in all activities, including making what are sometimes seen as tedious checks before taking action, is important.

PROBLEMS

16. You have a large team of 15 people who work in three groups each with their own leader. One of the group leaders is outstanding at his technical work. He is very good with clients. He is a good administrator and carries out his management tasks effectively. However, his people are not as well motivated as those in your other two groups. You believe that he has the potentiality to be a good leader as well as being a good manager. What can you do to help him?

17. For various reasons the demand for the services that your team has been providing has dropped significantly during the last 12 months. You are all making an effort to improve things. You have now come to the conclusion that you need to develop and launch a new service. It must be one that the team members have the skills to deliver. You want to involve your team colleagues in the process of formulating and implementing the new service. What are the main steps in this process?

18. You are worried about the quality of your team meetings. Your people like to subject minor matters to lengthy debates. There is a good deal of aggressive behaviour that is rationalized by claims 'to be playing the devil's advocate'. There is also a tendency for issues to be opened up again after decisions have been made. What can you do to put things right?

RECOMMENDED SOLUTIONS

16. This is another instance when coaching is likely to be helpful. You know that the group leader is very good with clients. That suggests that he has well-developed interpersonal skills. Your task, in the coaching session, is to raise his awareness of the fact that the interpersonal skills that he uses so well with his clients are exactly the same as those that can be used to good effect in leading his team. Once this has been grasped you could then explore the particular actions that he could take to be a more effective leader. Agree a plan of action for him to raise morale and foster team spirit. Have periodic review sessions.

17. Once again a good starting point for producing ideas and getting the team committed to the implementation of something new is a brainstorming session. When you feel that the team has produced some useful and interesting ideas then seek agreement on what should be done. New service proposals are likely to require further research and refinement. There may well be training implications. It would be useful to set up a small project team to turn the basic ideas into a new service proposal that is capable of being launched. Consider including, as members of the project team, not only some of your own people but one or two client representatives as well.

18. These time-wasting and frustrating forms of behaviour are usually symptoms of a lack of trust among team members. When this occurs people are not particularly open with each other and are less willing to contribute enthusiastically. They play games instead. Once you have decided that you need to build trust then I suggest that you take the team off-site and have a day's workshop. There are many trust-building exercises that can be undertaken, which involve the giving and receiving of feedback, soliciting everyone's views on when and why they trust others and developing codes of appropriate personal and team behaviour. You might wish to use a skilled facilitator for a workshop that is as important and sensitive as this in order to secure the best possible return for the team's considerable investment of time and effort.

PROBLEMS

19. You have had a very successful couple of years since you took on the leadership of your team. Everyone is pulling together and working hard. You have achieved your objectives and successfully launched two new services. The team has generated better profits than expected. Two days ago your most prestigious and profitable client told you that there would be no further business. The client had decided to switch to another provider. No reasons were given. You have decided to call your team members together. What will you tell them and what sort of discussion will you hold?

20. One of your senior team colleagues has had the responsibility for the last few months of supervising the work of two relatively new trainees. You have picked up some disquieting news on the grapevine. Both of the trainees are unhappy with the supervision that they have been getting. They get little guidance and virtually no feedback on their performance. How will you deal with this problem?

21. One of your team members has many first-class attributes but everybody agrees that he is a poor listener. When you and others have discussions with him he frequently glances at his watch, his eyes glaze over and he often fails to respond properly to questions. You feel that you should take the matter up with him and try to provide some help. What would be a good way to coach him?

RECOMMENDED SOLUTIONS

19. The loss of your most prestigious and profitable client will come as a great shock. It will be helpful to share everything that you know with your team members. Have a discussion on what may have gone wrong but be sure to avoid blaming anyone. The discussion needs to be concentrated on lessons that can be learnt for the future. Remind the team that you have other good clients and resolve to improve the quality of service that you provide to them. If you have enough information to help you then agree actions with your team members so that you reduce the risk of losing other clients.

20. Some leaders have difficulty in raising sensitive performance issues with senior colleagues. It is the mark of a good team leader that such matters are not ducked. A quiet word in the ear of the colleague who has the responsibility for supervising trainees is called for. You need to explain promptly what you have learnt on the grapevine and to ask your colleague what has been happening from his perspective. It is important to remind him that guidance and feedback for trainees is crucial for good motivation and performance. Furthermore a firm that has a reputation for supervising trainees well is more likely to attract high-quality people in the future. You may need to provide some help with the development of supervising skills.

21. The best time to deal with this tricky problem is when you are having a discussion and it becomes apparent to you that he is not listening. You could give some direct feedback. For example, say, 'We seem to be talking a lot but not making very much progress. Can you help me with this, please?' After getting a response and exploring it together, introduce some 'characteristics of good listeners' to the conversation. These could include, 'They look at the person talking, ask questions, indicate that they understand or agree, reflect back what has been said and, most important of all, give full attention.' Until they receive feedback poor listeners are often unaware that they have the problem. Once they realize that they could do better then they usually make the effort.

PROBLEMS

22. Your team is very successful. You have an excellent relationship with your team colleagues. You are aware that although they enjoy their work they are irritated by the fact that the firm's policy is not to disclose performance information to those who are not partners. You are not a partner and you share their irritation. You believe that the team would be better motivated if it were kept fully informed about the firm's progress. What is the best way for you to seek to get the firm's management board to change its mind on this issue and be willing to disseminate the information?

RECOMMENDED SOLUTIONS

22. A good team leader represents the interests of the team, with senior colleagues in the firm, when he or she believes it to be justified. There is ample evidence to show that keeping people informed about results and impending changes is generally good for morale and motivation and therefore performance. People are more likely to feel a sense of ownership. Take the matter up with the firm's top management. It will be useful to seek out colleagues who feel the same way as you do. Form an alliance with like-minded colleagues and make your representations together. Seek out one or two sympathetic senior people and discuss your intentions with them before raising the issue more formally. As in all efforts to influence others to do things differently, emphasize the benefits that will accrue to the firm and its people in having a change of policy.

References

Belbin, M (1981) *Management Teams: Why they succeed or fail*, Butterworth-Heinemann, London

Drucker, P (1989) *The New Realities*, Heinemann Professional, London

Fisher, Roger and Brown, Scott (1989) *Getting Together: Building a relationship that gets to yes*, Business Books, London

Fisher, R and Ury, W (1982) *Getting To Yes: Negotiating agreement without giving in*, Hutchinson, London

Goleman, D (1995) *Emotional Intelligence: Why it can matter more than IQ*, Bantam Books, New York

Hersey, P and Blanchard, K H (1993) *Management of Organizational Behaviour: Utilising human resources*, Prentice Hall, New Jersey

Herzberg, F (2003) One more time: how do you motivate employees?, *Harvard Business Review*, **81** (1), pp 87–96

Honey, P and Mumford, A (1992) *The Manual of Learning Styles*, Peter Honey, Maidenhead

Janis, I (1982) *Groupthink: Psychological studies of policy decisions and fiascoes*, Mifflin, Boston, MA

Jung, C J (1971) (first published in 1923) *The Collected Works of C.J. Jung*, vol 6, *Psychological Types*, Routledge & Kegan Paul, London

Kolb, D (1984) *Experiential Learning: Experience as the source of learning and development*, Prentice Hall, New Jersey

Kotter, J (1996) *Leading Change*, Harvard Business School Press, Boston, MA

Levinson, H (2003) Management by whose objectives?, *Harvard Business Review*, **81** (1), pp 107–16

Machiavelli, N (1999) (written originally *c* 1505) *The Prince*, Penguin Books, London

McCann, D (1988) *How to Influence Others at Work*, Heinemann Professional, London

Myers, I B (rev L K Kirby and K D Myers) (2000) *Introduction to Type: A guide to understanding your results on the Myers Briggs Type Indicator*, OPP, Oxford

Obeng, E (1994) *All Change: The project leader's secret handbook*, Financial Times Management, London

Orwell, G (1946) Politics and the English language, *Horizon* **76**

Osborn, A F (1953) *Applied Imagination: The principles and procedures of creative thinking*, Charles Scribner's Sons, New York

Scott, M (1992) *Time Management*, Century Business, London

Whitmore, J (1993) *Coaching for Performance*, Nicholas Brealey, London

Zander, R S and Zander, B (2000) *The Art of Possibility*, Penguin Books, London

Sources

Introduction
Digby Jones, Director-General, CBI: Correspondence

Chapter 1
Ed Smith, UK Board Member, PricewaterhouseCoopers: Interview
John Cridland, Deputy Director-General, CBI: Interview
Nigel Knowles, Managing Partner, DLA: Interview
Tim Solomon, Managing Partner, London Office, Ogilvy & Mather: Interview

Chapter 2
Richard Collier-Keywood, Partner, PricewaterhouseCoopers: Interview
David Law, Partner, PricewaterhouseCoopers: Interview
Chris Lucas, Partner, PricewaterhouseCoopers: Interview
Richard Sexton, Partner, PricewaterhouseCoopers: Interview
Alison Chadwick, Development Director, Abbott Mead Vickers: Interview

Chapter 3
John Stapleton, Managing Partner, Thomas Eggar: Interview
Robert Halton, Human Resources Director, DLA: Interview

Chapter 4
Nigel Knowles, Managing Partner, DLA: Interview
Tim Aspinall, Managing Partner, DMH: Interview

Chapter 5
Ian Pearman, Account Director, Abbott Mead Vickers: Interview
David Law, Partner, PricewaterhouseCoopers: Interview

Chapter 6
Chris Lucas, Partner, PricewaterhouseCoopers: Interview
Ed Smith, UK Board Member, PricewaterhouseCoopers: Interview
Tim Solomon, Managing Partner, London Office, Ogilvy & Mather: Interview
Alison Chadwick, Development Director, Abbott Mead Vickers: Interview
Ian Pearman, Account Director, Abbott Mead Vickers: Interview

Chapter 7
Paul Sharp, Head of Organization Development, Pricewaterhouse-Coopers: Interview
Ed Smith, UK Board Member, PricewaterhouseCoopers: Interview
Alison Chadwick, Development Director, Abbott Mead Vickers: Interview

Chapter 8
Nigel Knowles, Managing Partner, DLA: Interview
Richard Sexton, Partner, PricewaterhouseCoopers: Interview
Richard Collier-Keywood, Partner, PricewaterhouseCoopers: Interview
Jonathan Hood, Partner, Thomas Eggar: Correspondence
Ian Pearman, Account Director, Abbott Mead Vickers: Interview

Chapter 9
Tim Aspinall, Managing Partner, DMH: Interview
Cheryl Giovannoni, Chief Executive, Coley Porter Bell: Interview

Chapter 10
John Martin, Director - Clients and Markets, PricewaterhouseCoopers:
Correspondence
Denzil Jones, Personnel and Administration Director, DMH: Interview
Robert Halton, Human Resources Director, DLA: Interview

Chapter 11
Ed Smith, UK Board Member, PricewaterhouseCoopers: Interview
Robert Halton, Human Resources Director, DLA: Interview
Tim Solomon, Managing Partner, London Office, Ogilvy & Mather:
Interview

Chapter 12
Robert Halton, Human Resources Director, DLA: Interview
John Cridland, Deputy Director-General, CBI: Interview

Chapter 13
John Cridland, Deputy Director-General, CBI: Interview

Chapter 14
Cheryl Giovannoni, Chief Executive, Coley Porter Bell: Interview
Roger Harrison: Influencing styles questionnaire and explanatory notes

Index